Pennsylvania Bed & Breakfast Cookbook

Pennsylvania Bed & Breakfast Cookbook

First Edition
EAN 978-1-889593-18-0

Printed in China

Design: Katrina Girtakovska

Cover Photo: The Lafayette Inn, Easton, Pennsylvania
Courtesy of Jumping Rocks, Inc.

Back Cover Photo credits:
Top photo: Jumping Rocks, Inc.
Middle photo: Innkeeper, Keystone Inn
Bottom photo: Donna Chiarelli

The Bed & Breakfast Cookbook Series™ was originated by Carol Faino
& Doreen Hazledine of Peppermint Press in Denver, Colorado in 1996.

3D Press, Inc.
a Big Earth Publishing company
3005 Center Green Drive, Suite 220
Boulder, CO 80301

800-258-5830 (order toll free)
920-886-6674 (fax)
www.bigearthpublishing.com

Pennsylvania

The Keystone State had a key roll in the early formation of the young republic. During the Colonial times of the nation, the land of Pennsylvania was centrally located amidst the original 13 colonies. It became known as the Keystone State since it held the colonies together like a keystone or central stone in an arch that locks all of the other stones in place.

The state name of Pennsylvania means Penn's Woods. The Penn in Pennsylvania is not that of William Penn, the founder of Pennsylvania. It is actually named after Admiral William Penn's father who left his wealth and a significant piece of New World land to his son. This land was a debt payment to William Penn's father by King Charles II. The "Sylvania" in Pennsylvania means woodlands.

Pennsylvania is rich in American history. Who has not heard of George Washington and Valley Forge or the pivotal battle of the Civil War at Gettysburg? The state's motto is "Virtue, Liberty and Independence" and is well represented by one of the state's most prominent symbols, the Liberty Bell. In 1751, the Pennsylvania Assembly purchased the Bell to commemorate the 50-year anniversary of William Penn's 1701 Charter of Privileges, Pennsylvania's original Constitution. The Liberty Bell tolled to summon the residents of Philadelphia to hear the first public reading of the Declaration of Independence on July 8, 1776. In an effort to put an end to slavery in America, the Abolitionists adopted the Liberty Bell as their symbol for freedom.

Amish buggies, aprons and bonnets, red barns and silver silos, green rolling hills and acres of pumpkins create the imagery of rural Pennsylvania today. Major urban areas in the state include the cities of Philadelphia, Pittsburgh, Erie, and Harrisburg.

Slinky

STATE SYMBOLS

State Beverage: Milk
State Dog: Great Dane
State Animal: Whitetail Deer
State Flower: Mountain Laurel
State Tree: Hemlock

State Cookie: Chocolate Chip
State Fish: Brook Trout
State Game Bird: Ruffed Grouse
State Insect: Firefly
State Toy: Slinky

B. Franklin

FAMOUS PENNSYLVANIANS

William Penn
Betsy Ross
Benjamin Franklin
Jimmy & Tommy Dorsey
John Updike

Louisa May Alcott
Daniel Boone
Rachel Carson
W.C. Fields
Arnold Palmer

GEOGRAPHIC FEATURES OF NOTE

229 Miles of the Appalachian Trail
116 State Parks
20 State Forests with over 1.5 million acres
1 of the Great Lakes – Erie
4 Major River systems: Allegheny, Monongahela, Ohio
and Delaware
1 National Forest – the Allegheny with 500,000 acres

Mountain Laurel

A Pennsylvania Culinary Potpourri

PENNSYLVANIA ORIGINALS
Ice cream soda – 1874 by Robert M. Green
Root beer – 1876
Banana split – 1904 by Dr. David Strickler, pharmacist,
  Strickler's Drug Store in Latrobe
Bubble gum – 1928 by Richard James, Philadelphia
  (now made in Hollidaysburg)

PENNSYLVANIA FIRSTS
Pretzel factory – Julius Sturgis, Lititz, Lancaster County, 1784

PENNSYLVANIA'S BIGGEST
Chocolate factory – Hershey
Mushroom capital of the world – Kennett Square
Black cherry capital of the world – Kane

Ice Cream Soda

REGIONAL FOOD FAVORITES
PHILLY CHEESE STEAKS
In the Italian immigrant section of South Philadelphia, the Philly cheese steak was
born. Pat Olivieri, owner of Pat's King of Steaks, sold the usual sandwiches and hot
dogs until he had the idea for thinly sliced beef, gooey with cheese, resting on grilled
onions in an Italian roll. Pat Olivieri's grandson, Frank, carries on the tradition today
at Pat's King of Steaks. Philly customers even have their own local language with
which to order the cheesecake specialty: "cheesewit" means cheese with onions.

CITY CHICKEN
Western Pennsylvania is the home of city chicken. City chicken is a "mock" food.
It is a recipe that contains a foodstuff that may look like chicken and taste like chicken,
but which is definitely not chicken. It is named for an ingredient that is not in the recipe.
The earliest published recipe for city chicken is from 1946 and is made with pork
and veal.

SCRAPPLE
The word scrapple originates from the word "scrap." The scraps, in this case, refer
to unused pig parts mixed with cornmeal, onions, and a sprinkling of spices. Frugal
Pennsylvania Dutch farmers introduced scrapple into the Eastern Pennsylvania cuisine.
Today, no questionable pork parts are used in scrapple recipes. Scrapple fans garnish
their dishes with a variety of toppings: butter, maple syrup, applesauce, and ketchup are
some favorites. Scrapple is commonly served with eggs as a morning meal.

Other regional food favorites include:

Pretzel

Hoagies	Sticky Buns
Tastycakes	AP Cookies
Soft Pretzels	Lebanon Bolgna
Water Ice	Hershey's Chocolate
Stomboli	Shoofly Pie

Contents

Breads & Muffins

Breads
&
Muffins

The Inn on Maple Street

"The Family and Pet Friendly Bed & Breakfast"

One block from historic Route 6, in the mountains of northwest Pennsylvania's McKean County, you'll find the Inn on Maple Street. Cookies come fresh from the oven at this bed and breakfast, and fireflies dance on the lawn at night. Make your entrance through the unusual banker's door that has a stained-glass side panel in the prairie design of Frank Lloyd Wright. You'll see the stately old upright piano to appease guest's lyrical moods, and an impressive oak staircase. A classic chess set is ready for a match of wits in the Library Room. Shelves of paperbacks are for the taking, with a "take one, leave one" philosophy. The focus of the Parlor Room is on electronic entertainment and big bowls of popcorn. In each guestroom, you'll find tall windows with shutters and lace curtains, and a hand-crocheted afghan on every bed.

"...Outstanding Breakfast," is one guest's reaction to the breakfast buffet by candlelight in the Breakfast Room.

INNKEEPERS:	Jay D. Roush
ADDRESS:	115 Maple Street (one block off Route 6)
	Port Allegany, Pennsylvania 16743
TELEPHONE:	(814) 642-5171
E-MAIL:	innonmaplest@pennswoods.net
WEBSITE:	www.theinnonmaplestreet.com
ROOMS:	4 Rooms; 1 Suite; Private & shared baths
CHILDREN:	Welcome
PETS:	Welcome; Resident dog

Orange Tea Bread

Makes 3 Loaves

"This dense quick bread tastes better if it sits for a day.
Drizzle the tops of the loaves with melted, semi-sweet chocolate
before slicing." ~ Innkeeper, Inn on Maple Street

4	**cups flour**
1/4	**cup orange zest, freshly grated**
2	**teaspoons cinnamon**
4	**teaspoons baking powder**
2	**sticks butter (real butter only)**
1	**cup white sugar**
1	**cup brown sugar, packed**
4	**large eggs**
1	**cup orange juice**
1	**cup plain or orange flavored yogurt**
2	**teaspoons orange or vanilla extract**
3/4	**cup semi-sweet chocolate chips, melted**

Preheat oven to 350°F. Heavily grease or butter 3 9½ x 5-inch loaf pans. Sift the flour, orange zest, cinnamon, and baking powder in a medium bowl. Combine butter, white and brown sugar, eggs, juice, yogurt, and orange or vanilla extract in a large bowl. Beat with a mixer for 5 minutes. Set the mixer on low speed and mix in flour just until blended. Divide the batter among loaf pans.

Bake batter on center rack of oven for 45-50 minutes or until tops are browned. Cool; drizzle chocolate across tops of loaves. Let stand for one day for flavors to develop; slice and serve.

Casa DaCosta

There is a dramatic view of the Mercer County Courthouse from the outdoor patio at the Casa DaCosta Bed & Breakfast. A baby grand piano, a marble-inlaid fireplace, and a crystal chandelier create a lovely view for the guests who are lounging on camelback sofas in the living room. The Victoria, Belle Vista, and Shenandoah guestrooms allow one to feel that it's yesterday once more.

Cheese strata and lemon poppy scones are two of the breakfast specialties served to the guests staying in this two-story, brick, Greek-revival home. Inquire about the tea parties for groups of four to fifteen. Sample the delicate finger sandwiches and sweet pastries, accompanied by your choice of tea. Gift baskets are available upon request.

"This house was built in 1929 by Lucille Webster, whom
we like to fancy still roams the halls." ~Innkeeper

INNKEEPERS:	Caroline L. DaCosta
ADDRESS:	116 West Market Street
	Mercer, Pennsylvania 16137
TELEPHONE:	(724) 662-5681; (888) 824-3763
E-MAIL:	casadacosta@zoominternet.net
WEBSITE:	www.casadacosta.net
ROOMS:	2 Rooms; 1 Suite; Private and shared baths
CHILDREN:	Unable to accommodate
PETS:	Not allowed; Resident dog

Aunt Wilda's Banana Breads

Makes 3 Small Loaves

"This can be mixed by hand; so simple a child can do it. I always send a loaf home with guests. My aunt, a cook for a restaurant, developed this recipe."
~ Innkeeper, Casa DaCosta Bed & Breakfast

½	**cup butter, melted**
1	**cup sugar**
2	**eggs**
2	**cups flour**
1	**teaspoon baking soda**
3	**ripe bananas, mashed with fork**
¼	**cup walnuts**

Cream cheese, for garnish

Preheat oven to 350°F. Cream melted butter and sugar. Stir in eggs. Add flour and soda; mix. Add bananas and nuts; mix. Pour into 3 small ungreased baking pans. Bake for 40-50 minutes.

Cool on wire racks and serve with cream cheese.

Flowers & Thyme

All variations of the colors lavender and pink enhance the acre of countryside that is home to Flowers & Thyme. From early spring until late fall, perennial flowers mixed with annuals, plus the herb gardens create a colorful and lush vision for guests of the inn. "We've been featured in the *Birds & Blooms* magazine, but it's the thoughtful comments from our guests that we cherish the most," say the innkeepers.

Built in 1941, the brick Colonial house was constructed by an Amish man for a Mennonite family. Cheery, eclectic furnishings lend an air of elegant simplicity to Flowers & Thyme. The large, commodious Gathering Room has a vaulted ceiling and an expanse of windows overlooking a peaceful valley with a working farm. Bountiful breakfasts are served in this room.
Aromas from snow pea garden breakfast quiche, French toast with southern fried apples, or eggs scrambled with a rich chicken sauce may be wafting through the inn as you awaken.

INNKEEPERS:	Don and Ruth Harnish
ADDRESS:	238 Strasburg Pike
	Lancaster, Pennsylvania 17602
TELEPHONE:	(717) 393-1460
E-MAIL:	Innkeeper@flowersandthyme.com
WEBSITE:	www.flowersandthyme.com
ROOMS:	3 Rooms; Private baths
CHILDREN:	Age 12 and older welcome
PETS:	Not allowed

Best Ever Banana Nut Bread

Makes 6 Servings

"I took several banana bread recipes and came up with this one."
~ Innkeeper, Flowers & Thyme Bed & Breakfast

¾	cup plus 2 tablespoons flour
½	cup sugar
½	teaspoon baking soda
¼	teaspoon salt
1	egg
1	ripe banana, mashed
¼	cup vegetable oil
⅛	cup buttermilk
¼	teaspoon vanilla extract
½	cup nuts, chopped

Preheat oven to 325°F. Sift the flour, sugar, baking soda, and salt into a large bowl. In a medium bowl, combine egg, banana, oil, buttermilk, and vanilla; mix well. Add egg mixture to flour mixture and stir just until flour mixture is moistened. Fold in nuts. Pour batter into a greased 2½ x 5-inch mini loaf pan. Bake for 40-45 minutes until a toothpick inserted in the center of the bread comes out clean.

Belle Reve

"Where a Dream and a River Meet" is the innkeeper's slogan for Belle Reve, an historic riverside bed and breakfast in the Village of Riverton.

The Delaware River is an amenity for travelers staying at the inn. Many of the rooms in this 1843 Greek Revival farmhouse have river views. The riverfront gazebo invites guests to while away the hours. A new Belle Reve dock on the banks of the Delaware provides the perfect stopover opportunity for river kayakers The bed and breakfast is at the foot of a bridge that leads to the tiny town of Belvidere. Walk or bicycle across the span, and you'll find a pretty-as-a-picture-postcard blend of finely maintained Colonial and Victorian mansions. The winter holiday lights are exquisite at the Belle Reve. Of course, the sparkling lights are multiplied by their reflection on the Delaware River.

INNKEEPERS:	Shirley K. Creo
ADDRESS:	7757 Martins Creek-Belvidere Road
	Bangor, Pennsylvania 18013
TELEPHONE:	(610) 498-2026; (888) 549-8608
E-MAIL:	bellereve@enter.net
WEBSITE:	www.bellereveriverside.com
ROOMS:	4 Rooms; 1 Suite; Private baths
CHILDREN:	Age 14 and older welcome
PETS:	Not allowed

Banana Nut Loaf

Makes 8 Servings

$\frac{1}{2}$	cup shortening
1	cup sugar
2	eggs, beaten
3	ripe bananas, mashed
2	cups flour
1	teaspoon salt
1	teaspoon baking soda dissolved in 3 tablespoons cold water
1	teaspoon vanilla
$\frac{1}{2}$	cup nuts or chocolate chips (both optional)

Preheat oven to 325°F. Cream shortening and sugar. Add eggs and mashed bananas. Add flour, salt, and the baking soda water. Fold in vanilla and nuts. Pour into a loaf pan approximately 11 x 4½ x 2¾ inches.

Bake for 1 hour.

Hickory Bridge Farm

At the base of the foothills of the Appalachian Mountains, sits the Hickory Bridge Farm. A well-stocked trout stream winds through the farm, which is nine miles west of Gettysburg. Farm-related antiques decorate the late-1700s farmhouse, where deer can be spotted from the large deck in the backyard. Quiet country cottages are positioned in the woods by the creek. A full breakfast is featured Monday through Saturday at the farmhouse, and Continental breakfast baskets are prepared for guests on Sunday.

Since 1977, delicious, bountiful dinners have been served in the restored 180-year-old barn. Linen tablecloths are often adorned with fresh flowers from the garden. The main course of the dinner is presented family-style at your own table, and consists of three entrees, several vegetables, corn fritters, and stewed apples. There is always dessert, and the dessert is always homemade.

INNKEEPERS:	Mary Lynn and Robert Martin
ADDRESS:	96 Hickory Bridge Road
	Orrtanna, Pennsylvania 17353
TELEPHONE:	(717) 642-5261; (800) 642-1766
E-MAIL:	hickory@pa.net
WEBSITE:	www.hickorybridgefarm.com
ROOMS:	7 Rooms; 6 Private baths
CHILDREN:	Welcome; Call ahead
PETS:	Not allowed

Old Fashioned Potato Bread

Makes 12 to 14 Servings

"...Another one of our restaurant's traditions."
~ Innkeeper, Hickory Bridge Farm

1	medium potato; washed, pared, and cut into pieces
2	tablespoons butter or margarine
2	packages of dry yeast
2	tablespoons sugar
2	teaspoons salt
1	cup milk, slightly warm
$5\frac{1}{2}$ - 6	cups flour

Preheat oven to 375°F. Cook potato in a small amount of water until tender; drain and reserve liquid.

Mash potato and measure ¾ cup; set aside. Add enough water to reserved liquid to make 1 cup; cool to 105-115°F. In a large mixing bowl, dissolve yeast in the potato liquid. Add butter, and stir well. Stir in sugar, salt, milk, mashed potatoes, and 1 cup flour. Gradually stir in enough flour to make the dough stiff. Turn dough out onto a floured surface, and knead until smooth and elastic, about 8 minutes. Place in a well greased bowl, turning the dough to grease dough's surface. Cover and let rise in a warm place, free from drafts, for 1 hour or until doubled. Punch down dough, and divide in half; shape each into a loaf. Place in 2 well greased 8x4x3-inch pans. Cover and let rise until doubled, about 30 minutes.

Bake for 25 minutes or until the loaves sound hollow when tapped.

Cresson House

The spacious grounds of the classic Colonial Cresson House are just minutes away from I-99, and 180 miles northwest of Washington D.C. This tastefully decorated inn is nestled in the Allegheny Mountains of Central Pennsylvania.

The Cresson area is a popular destination for railroad buffs: Tunnels Park and Museum is immediately adjacent to the Gallitzen Tunnels; the Heritage Park observation platform, and Pennsylvania Railroad Caboose are in Derry. Nearby Altoona is home to the Horseshoe Curve National Historic Landmark and the Railroader's Memorial Museum. Another local attraction, the Mount Assisi Gardens, is cultivated on the palatial grounds of former steel baron Charles Schwab. The Franciscans who now occupy the mansion maintain this Italian formal garden.

INNKEEPERS:	Marti Stefanon
ADDRESS:	417 Park Avenue
	Cresson, Pennsylvania 16630
TELEPHONE:	(814) 886-5014
E-MAIL:	cressonhouse@verizon.net
WEBSITE:	www.cressonhouse.com
ROOMS:	5 Rooms; Private bath
CHILDREN:	Welcome
PETS:	Not allowed

Cinnamon Pecan Rolls

Makes 12 Servings

"This recipe was given to me many years ago."
~ Innkeeper, Cresson House Bed & Breakfast

1	**loaf sweet dough, thawed**
3	**tablespoons butter or margarine, melted**
½	**cup brown sugar, divided**
2	**teaspoons water**
2	**tablespoons light corn syrup**
½	**cup pecan halves**
2	**tablespoons cinnamon**

Preheat oven to 350°F. Grease a 9x13-inch pan with 1 tablespoon of butter. Combine 2 tablespoons butter, ¼ cup brown sugar, water, and corn syrup. Spread in the pan. Sprinkle with pecans.

Roll dough on oiled surface into a 16x12-inch rectangle. Sprinkle with remaining ¼ cup brown sugar and cinnamon. Roll up starting at 16-inch side. Cut into 12 pieces.

Bake for 15-20 minutes. Cool 1 minute, then loosen edges and turn out onto a waxed paper lined wire rack.

Keller House

The Keller family occupied this home in the farm country of Penn Valley for over ninety years. The Keller House was built in 1887, in the village of Centre Valley. Your hosts at the Keller House today, Ernie and Kathy Mowery, beckon travelers to join them in the sitting room to share the old-fashioned pleasure of the Edison Victrola.

Later in the evening, retire to the Romance Room with a private Jacuzzi for two. Or, choose the General's Hideaway with pictures of Civil War era generals adorning both bedroom and bathroom. Melt your cares away as you soak in the antique claw-foot bathtub in the Garden Suite.

Your morning fare will be presented on china and crystal, once used by the Keller family. A couple of The Keller House breakfast favorites are Ernie's Famous Sausage Peach Puff Pancakes, and the Egg'stra Special Breakfast Casserole.

INNKEEPERS:	Ernie and Kathy Mowery
ADDRESS:	109 West Church Street
	Centre Hall, Pennsylvania 16828
TELEPHONE:	(814) 364-2225; (888) 554-2588
E-MAIL:	info@kellerhousebb.com
WEBSITE:	www.kellerhousebb.com
ROOMS:	4 Rooms; 1 Suites; Private baths
CHILDREN:	Age 13 and older welcome
PETS:	Not allowed

Apple Muffins

Makes 12 Muffins

1½	cups brown sugar, firmly packed
⅔	cup olive oil
1	egg
1	cup buttermilk
1	teaspoon salt
1	teaspoon baking soda
1	teaspoon vanilla extract
2	cups flour
1½	cups apples, chopped (Granny Smith or Red Delicious)
½	cup nuts, chopped

Preheat oven to 350°F. Mix brown sugar, oil, and egg. Combine buttermilk, salt, baking soda, and vanilla and mix thoroughly into egg mixture. Add flour. Fold in apples and nuts.

Pour into greased muffin cups and bake for 30 minutes.

Carter Camp Lodge

"One of Nature's Last Outposts"

Located in downtown Carter Camp, population 2, the lodge has provided food and accommodations for wayward travelers for over 150 years. Built in the 1850s as a stagecoach stop, the exterior of the lodge is much as it was at the turn of the century. There are seven guest rooms on the second floor. A sitting room and a large dining area are available for guests to gather and socialize, or relax by the woodstove and unwind. Carter Camp Lodge Café serves a full country breakfast. The store, also on the premises, offers locally produced items, sporting goods, and groceries.

Do you like to hike? Are you tired of carrying your backpack? Use a goat! Goats are coming soon to Carter Camp to help carry your gear.

INNKEEPERS:	John and Barbara Andrews
ADDRESS:	2136 Germania Road
	Galeton, Pennsylvania 16922
TELEPHONE:	(814) 435-1192
E-MAIL:	Not Available
WEBSITE:	www.cartercamplodge.com
ROOMS:	7 Rooms; Private and Shared baths
CHILDREN:	Welcome
PETS:	Not allowed; Resident dog and cat

Cappuccino Muffins

Makes 8 to 12 Cupcake Size or 6 Large Muffin Size Servings

Adapted from *Country Inn & Bed & Breakfast*

1¾	cups flour
⅓	cup brown sugar
1	tablespoon baking powder
¼	teaspoon salt
½	cup chocolate chips
1	egg
¾	cup milk
2	tablespoons instant coffee
1	teaspoon vanilla extract
½	cup melted butter
½	cup cinnamon chips

Preheat oven to 375°F. Combine the first 5 ingredients in a large bowl. Combine the egg, milk, coffee, and vanilla in a small bowl. With a whisk, beat the liquid until the instant coffee is dissolved. Mix the egg mixture and melted butter into the dry ingredients. Mix until the dry ingredients are moist. Pour the batter into greased muffin tins, filling to ¾ of each cup.

Sprinkle tops with cinnamon chips.

Bake for 18-20 minutes.

Pheasant Field

The three-acre pond and island, along with ten acres of farmland, is the habitat for bullfrogs, geese, and songbirds to create a symphony on summer evenings at the Pheasant Field Bed and Breakfast. Your accommodations are provided in the 200-year-old central Pennsylvania brick farmhouse. The family room, once the summer kitchen, was used as a stop on the Underground Railroad.

An inviting dining room welcomes you for a country breakfast, served at your convenience from 5:30 to 10:30 A.M. on most mornings. On-site tennis courts at Pheasant Field offer the perfect opportunity for you to practice your backhand. During your visit you can stable your horse in the historic stone barn. Pastures and run-in sheds are also available. The Appalachian Trail is less than a mile away. Maps of hiking routes on the Trail, as well as menus from area restaurants, are conveniently on hand at the bed and breakfast.

INNKEEPERS:	Dee Segan and Chuck DeMarco
ADDRESS:	150 Hickorytown Road
	Carlisle, Pennsylvania 17013
TELEPHONE:	(717) 258-0717; (877) 258-0717
E-MAIL:	stay@pheasantfield.com
WEBSITE:	www.pheasantfield.com
ROOMS:	7 Rooms; 2 Suites; 1 Cottage; Private baths
CHILDREN:	Age 8 and older welcome
PETS:	Dogs, cats and horses welcome with limited availability

Morning Glory Muffins

Makes 12 Large or 18 Medium Muffin Size Servings

Adapted from *The American Country Inn and Bed & Breakfast Cookbook Vol. 2*

"This is a recipe that is often requested by guests."
~ *Innkeeper, Pheasant Field Bed & Breakfast*

2	cups flour
1¼	cups sugar
2	teaspoons baking soda
2	teaspoons cinnamon
3	eggs, beaten
1	cup vegetable oil
2	teaspoons vanilla extract
2	cups carrot, grated
1	apple, grated
½	cup raisins
½	cup pecans or walnuts, chopped
½	cup coconut

Preheat oven to 375°F. Grease muffin cups.

In a large bowl, combine flour, sugar, baking soda, and cinnamon. In a small bowl, combine eggs, oil, and vanilla.

Add egg mixture to flour mixture and stir until flour mixture is moistened. Fold in carrot, apple, raisins, pecans, and coconut. Spoon batter into muffin cups and bake for 25 minutes.

Aaron Burr House

The Aaron Burr House takes its name from the third vice president of the United States. After Aaron Burr's infamous and fatal pistol duel with Alexander Hamilton in 1804, Burr escaped to New Hope seeking a safe haven. The inn's foundation is all that remains of the original pre-Revolutionary War era home where Burr is said to have hidden for a week. Today, the Aaron Burr house provides a warm and friendly atmosphere for weary city dwellers seeking escape to rural Bucks County.

> *"Wow! I had a fight with my honey the same week, but 200 years apart from Burr's duel with Hamilton. The Burr and Hamilton families took 200 years to end their feud. With the help of this big, lace canopy bed, we kissed and made up in two minutes. New Hope is for lovers, and the Aaron Burr House is the best place to kiss." ~ Guest*

The tree-shaded corner location and the large, screened-in flagstone patio reflect the peaceful atmosphere at the Aaron Burr House. "Fresh is best" is the innkeepers' motto regarding breakfast.

INNKEEPERS:	Jess and Nadine Sill
ADDRESS:	80 West Bridge Street
	New Hope Boro, Pennsylvania 18938
TELEPHONE:	(215) 862-2520
E-MAIL:	stay@aaronburrhouse.com
WEBSITE:	www.aaronburrhouse.com
ROOMS:	6 Rooms; 1 Suite; 1 Cottage; Private baths
CHILDREN:	Age 12 and older welcome
PETS:	Not allowed

Coconut Orange Tea Muffins

Makes 12 Muffins

$1\frac{1}{2}$	cups flour
$\frac{1}{2}$	cup sugar
2	teaspoons baking powder
$\frac{1}{2}$	teaspoon salt
$\frac{1}{2}$	cup butter or margarine
Zest of 2 oranges	
$\frac{1}{2}$	cup orange juice
2	large eggs
$\frac{1}{2}$	cup sweetened and flaked coconut plus $\frac{1}{4}$ cup, for garnish

Preheat oven to 375°F. Grease 12 $2\frac{1}{2}$-inch muffin cups. In a large bowl, mix flour, sugar, baking powder, and salt until well blended. Melt butter in a medium sauce pan; remove from heat. Stir in orange zest, orange juice, and eggs until well blended.

Add coconut and stir into the flour mixture just until moistened. Spoon the batter into the prepared muffin cups. Sprinkle the extra coconut on top of each muffin. Bake approximately 22-25 minutes until the muffins are lightly golden around the edges.

The Boothby Inn

"I have stayed at B & B's, small inns and guest houses from coast to coast and continent to continent, I have never described one as perfect ~ until now. Congratulations! Beauty, utility, and amenities coupled with hospitality to make this that stay one searches for." ~ Guest

When you open the front door, you enter into a spectacular hall with the original wood stairway and stained glass windows. Expect a warm greeting, sounds of classical music, fires in the fireplaces, and pampering in the wondrous guest rooms. The accommodations at The Boothby Inn are professionally decorated with an international theme. Would you prefer the France, Japan, Scotland, or Africa Room? On warm mornings, breakfast may be served on the garden patio. Savor the most luxurious accommodations in downtown Erie and count on a very memorable stay.

INNKEEPERS:	Gloria Knox
ADDRESS:	311 West Sixth Street
	Erie, Pennsylvania 16507
TELEPHONE:	(814) 456-1888; (866) 266-8429
E-MAIL:	info@theboothbyinn.com
WEBSITE:	www.theboothbyinn.com
ROOMS:	4 Rooms; Private baths
CHILDREN:	Age 12 and older welcome
PETS:	Not allowed

English Muffin Loaves

Makes 12 to 14 Servings

"Easy, great to do ahead, and freezes well" ~ Innkeeper, Boothby Inn

5½	cups flour
2	packages yeast
1	tablespoon sugar
2	teaspoons salt
¼	teaspoon baking soda
2	cups milk
½	cup water
⅛	cup cornmeal

Preheat oven to 375°F. Combine 3 cups of flour, yeast, sugar, salt, and baking soda in a mixing bowl. Heat the liquids until very warm, 120-130°F. Add milk and water to dry mixture. Use the mixer's paddle attachment to beat well. Stir in remaining 2½ cups of flour to make a stiff batter. Spoon the batter into 2 8½ x 4½-inch bread pans that have been greased and sprinkled with cornmeal. Sprinkle cornmeal on top.

Cover and let rise for 45 minutes. Bake for 30 minutes.

Tara – A Country Inn

Inspired by the movie, *Gone With the Wind*, Tara – A Country Inn, offers you a lasting impression of southern hospitality. Innkeepers Donna and Jim Winner are passionate *Gone With the Wind* historians. One of their prized acquisitions displayed at the inn is the robe worn by actress Vivian Leigh during the honeymoon scene in the movie.

This 1854 mansion has twenty-seven luxurious guestrooms with fireplaces and Jacuzzis. A view of the 450-acre Shenango Lake; Frederick Remington bronze statuary within Tara's impressive formal gardens; a heated swimming pool; complimentary bicycles; and gourmet and casual dining are just a few of the special amenities. Tara is a virtual museum of Civil War and *Gone With the Wind* memorabilia. Tours with the knowledgeable inn guides are encouraged. As a setting for romantic getaways, weddings, meetings, or private parties, it is ideal.

INNKEEPERS:	Donna and Jim Winner
ADDRESS:	2844 Lake Road
	Clark, Pennsylvania 16113
TELEPHONE:	(724) 962-3535; (800) 782-2803
E-MAIL:	info@tara-inn.com
WEBSITE:	www.tara-inn.com
ROOMS:	24 Rooms; 3 Suites; Private baths
CHILDREN:	Age 12 and older welcome
PETS:	Not allowed

Sue Ellen's Strudel Muffins

Makes 12 Servings

"Many recipes, including this one, have been staples on Tara's breakfast menu since 1986." ~ Innkeeper, Tara – A Country Inn

2	cups flour
½	cup sugar
2	teaspoons baking powder
½	teaspoon salt
½	cup butter, softened
1	cup red apple, peeled and cubed
1	large egg
⅔	cup milk
½	cup dry ingredients/butter mixture reserved from above
1	tablespoon sugar
¼	cup walnuts, chopped

Preheat oven to 425°F. Combine flour, sugar, baking powder, and salt in a mixing bowl. Add softened butter and stir. Remove ¼ cup of mixture and set aside for topping. Add apples, egg, and milk. Stir until well blended. Spoon into 2½-inch greased muffin tins. Sprinkle the topping mixture the over the muffin batter. Bake for 20 minutes.

House at the End of the Road

The House at the End of the Road is a pre-1900 farmhouse tucked away from time and traffic on twenty-five wooded acres in the western Pennsylvania town of Summerville. The Inn's Willow Bedroom looks out on the 100-year-old willow tree and the original post-and-beam barn. Bring your fly-fishing gear and try your luck in the Redbank Creek, or simply take a walk along its banks. Play target golf, horseshoes, or take advantage of the 30-foot–by-60-foot athletic court to practice your jump shot or volleyball serve.

The 8,500-acre Cook Park National Forest is nearby. The area is famous for its old growth forest, once referred to as the "Black Forest." Cook Park's "Forest Cathedral" of magnificent lofty hemlocks and white pines is a National Natural Landmark. Along the eastern border of the park, canoeing and rafting on the Clarion River is a favorite pastime.

INNKEEPERS:	Pam and David Henderson
ADDRESS:	518 Bauer Road
	Summerville, Pennsylvania 15864
TELEPHONE:	(814) 856-3480; (800) 905-6647
E-MAIL:	info@thehouseattheendoftheroad.com
WEBSITE:	www.houseatheendoftheroad.com
ROOMS:	2 Suites; Private baths
CHILDREN:	Unable to accommodate
PETS:	Not allowed

Muffins That Taste Like Donuts

Makes 12 Muffins

1¾	cups flour
1½	teaspoons baking powder
½ ¼	teaspoon salt
½	teaspoon nutmeg
¼	teaspoon cinnamon
⅓	cup oil
¾	cup sugar
1	egg
¾	cup milk

Melted butter, for garnish
Sugar and cinnamon mixture, for garnish

Preheat oven to 350°F. Mix all dry ingredients in a bowl. Mix all wet ingredients in a separate bowl. Combine dry and wet ingredients just until blended. Don't over mix. Pour the batter into a muffin pan.

19

Bake for 15 minutes. While the muffins are still hot, dip the muffin top in melted butter, and then dip the butter topped muffin into a mixture of sugar and cinnamon. *Spread butter on top with knife.*
Allow to melt; sprinkle with c/s mix.

Dillweed

Dillweed Bed and Breakfast is a turn-of-the-century home built by the Dill family, early settlers of Dilltown. Antique hats, hatpins, vintage clothing, and antique toys are all part of the decor in the four guestrooms and the Garden Suite. The rooms have the charming names of Parsley, Sage, Rosemary, and Thyme. The Parsley Room has a particularly good view of Dillweed's herb garden. The on-site Trailside Shop offers two floors of country gifts and antiques for your browsing pleasure.

Dillweed is located at the beginning of Ghost Town Trail, an historic rail-trail project. The limestone-surfaced trail passes by once-thriving mining communities, following Blacklick Creek. The Ghost Town Trail is a multi-use recreational trail appropriate for hiking, biking, horseback riding, and cross-country skiing.

INNKEEPERS:	Corey, Kyra and Cindy Gilmore
ADDRESS:	PO Box 1
	Dilltown, Pennsylvania 15929
TELEPHONE:	(814) 446-6465
E-MAIL:	dillweed@floodcity.net
WEBSITE:	www.dillweedinc.com
ROOMS:	4 Rooms; 1 Suite; Private and shared baths
CHILDREN:	Welcome
PETS:	Not allowed

Cheddar Dill Scones

Makes 12 Scones

3	cups flour
2	tablespoons sugar
3	teaspoons salt
1	tablespoon plus 1 teaspoon baking powder
$\frac{1}{3}$	cup dill, coarsely chopped
$1\frac{1}{3}$	cups sharp cheddar cheese, finely grated
$1\frac{2}{3}$	cups heavy whipping cream

Preheat oven to 425°F. Sift flour, sugar, salt, and baking powder into a large bowl and whisk. Add dill and 1 cup of cheddar cheese; continue to whisk. Add cream, and stir until it is a dough-like consistency, but still lumpy. Knead dough gently. Transfer dough to a floured surface and pat into 10-inch circle with the dough twice as thick in the middle as it is at the edge. Sprinkle remaining cheese on top.

Cut into 12 pie wedges. Put wedges on an ungreased baking sheet.

Bake 12-15 minutes until lightly browned. Top with heavy whipping cream.

Jacob's Resting Place

Built two centuries ago as a colonial tavern-inn called The Sign of the Green Tree, this pristine brick Georgian offered respite to travelers. Now, Jacob's Resting Place occupies the same quarters on the same three acres at the edge of Carlisle. Trout continue to thrive in the Letort stream that is on the property.

In the formal foursquare garden, the brick walkways are Jeffersonian in design, and are lined with American Boxwood. The octagonal cottage garden is filled with medicinal and culinary herbs, dye plants, and ornamentals. The center area garden is covered with oyster shells that were dug while planting the garden. Oysters brought up the Susquehanna River were a staple on the original tavern menu. After serving, the shells were tossed out the back door where they remained for 200 years.

Terry Heglin, present-day innkeeper at Jacob's Resting Place, is a Civil War historian, and a wonderful resource to tap before a trip to the nearby Military History Institute.

INNKEEPERS:	Terry and Marie Hegglin
ADDRESS:	1007 Harrisburg Pike
	Carlisle, Pennsylvania 17013
TELEPHONE:	(717) 243-1766; (888) 731-1790
E-MAIL:	jacobsrest@pa.net
WEBSITE:	www.jacobsrestingplace.com
ROOMS:	5 Rooms; 4 Suites; Private baths
CHILDREN:	Age 12 and older welcome
PETS:	Not allowed

Cream Filled Pumpkin Bread

Makes 8 Servings

Bread:

2⅔	cups sugar
2	cups canned pumpkin
⅔	cup water
4	eggs
⅔	cup oil
3½	cups flour
½	teaspoon baking powder
1	teaspoon cinnamon
1	teaspoon ginger
1¾	teaspoons salt
2	teaspoons baking soda
1	cup nuts, chopped
1	cup raisins

Cream Filling:

8	ounces cream cheese
½	cup sugar
1	egg
1	tablespoon flour
½	teaspoon nutmeg

Preheat oven to 350°F. Mix all bread (first 13) ingredients. Pour ½ of the bread batter into a greased bundt pan. In a separate bowl, mix the ingredients for the cream filling. Pour the filling over the first layer of the bread batter. Pour the remainder of the bread batter on top.

Bake for 60 minutes.

Mill Creek Homestead

The Mill Creek Homestead stands along a two-lane country road in the village of Bird-in-Hand. The 1793 stone house is accented by towering pine trees that limit a distant view, but you may see Amish neighbors working in their tobacco or cornfields or hanging tobacco in the barn to dry. Guests in the otherwise enveloping silence will probably notice the sound of horse and buggies passing by.

Many visitors inquire about the origination of the village name, Bird-in-Hand. At the time that Old Philadelphia Pike was being laid out between Lancaster and Philadelphia, road surveyors were making McNabb's Hotel their headquarters. The sign in front of the inn portrayed a man with a bird in his hand, and the hotel soon became known as the Bird-in-Hand Inn. This hotel designation became the landmark identifying the area. Variations of the original sign appear throughout the town today.

INNKEEPERS:	Vicki and Frank Alfone
ADDRESS:	2578 Old Philadelphia Pike
	Bird-in-Hand (Lancaster County) Pennsylvania 17505
TELEPHONE:	(717) 291-6419; (8000 771-2578
E-MAIL:	millcreekbnb@hotmail.com
WEBSITE:	www.millcreekhomestead.com
ROOMS:	4 Rooms; Private baths
CHILDREN:	Age 10 and older welcome
PETS:	Not allowed

Ricotta Pineapple Muffins

Makes 12 Muffins

"Great to keep in the freezer and then warm for a quick breakfast treat."
~ Innkeeper, Mill Creek Homestead Bed & Breakfast

1	egg
¼	cup oil
1½	cups ricotta cheese
2	cups flour
½	cup sugar
1	tablespoon baking powder
½	teaspoon baking soda
1	cup pineapple, crushed
¼	cup toasted coconut, for topping (optional)

Preheat the oven to 375°F. Mix egg, oil, and cheese until smooth. Add dry ingredients and mix. Stir in crushed pineapple. Fill 12 muffin cups and top with coconut, if desired.

Bake for 25 minutes.

Coffee Cakes & Cereals

Coffee Cakes

&

Cereals

Country Farmhouse

S et the mood for a peaceful stay by playing soft music on the 1860s pump organ in the parlor of the 1834 stone Country Farmhouse. Fresh flowers, a handmade Amish quilt on your bed, and soap—homemade by the innkeeper— will be waiting for you in your room. Wake to the smell of fresh-ground coffee. The Country Farmhouse has their own house blend that is roasted especially for their guests.

T he old summer kitchen has been restored and reborn as a romantic cottage with a walk-in fireplace and a whirlpool tub. Walk through the winding paths of the cottage garden, and delight your senses with its many specimens of hollyhocks, dahlias, gladiolas, hibiscus, and roses. The comfortable tree swing is a great place for bird watching. Right around the corner, there is a walking trail that meanders along a trout preservation stream. What a wonderful place to view the swaying corn and wheat fields, or to befriend the neighboring cows.

INNKEEPERS:	Barb and Terry Stephens
ADDRESS:	1780 Donegal Springs Road
	Mount Joy, Pennsylvania 17552
TELEPHONE:	(717) 653-0935; (866) 653-0935
E-MAIL:	brguest@countryfarmhouse.net
WEBSITE:	www.countryfarmhouse.net
ROOMS:	2 Rooms; 1 Cottage; Private baths
CHILDREN:	Unable to accommodate
PETS:	Not allowed

Overnight Blueberry Coffee Cake

Makes 8 Servings

"This coffee cake must be refrigerated overnight."
~ Innkeeper, Country Farmhouse Bed & Breakfast

1	egg
$\frac{1}{2}$	cup plus 2 tablespoons sugar
$1\frac{1}{4}$	cups flour
2	teaspoons baking powder
$\frac{3}{4}$	teaspoon salt
$\frac{1}{3}$	cup milk
3	tablespoons butter or margarine, melted
1	cup fresh blueberries

In a mixing bowl, beat egg and $\frac{1}{2}$ cup sugar. In a separate bowl, combine flour, baking powder, and salt; add alternately with milk to sugar mixture, beating well after each addition. Stir in butter. Fold in berries. Pour into a greased 8-inch square baking pan. Sprinkle with remaining sugar.
Cover and chill overnight.

Remove from refrigerator 30 minutes before baking.

Preheat oven to 350°F. Bake for 30-35 minutes.

Buhl Mansion Guesthouse & Spa

One of America's most luxurious bed and breakfasts, Buhl Mansion is listed on the National Register of Historic Places. This 1890s castle offers 10 opulent guestrooms with fireplaces, Jacuzzi's, the finest amenities, and royal service.

The grand, oak staircase that ascends to the second and third floors is used to reach the guest rooms. A hand-painted mural of formal gardens and cherubs welcomes you on the third level. Buhl Mansion is home to a splendid art gallery of original oil paintings, bronze statuary, and magnificent antiques. The full-service spa, with nearly 100 indulgent spa treatments available, provides the ultimate in luxury and pampering. The Buhl Mansion is perfect for romantic getaways and executive retreats. The Victorian greenhouse, carriage house, and formal gardens provide a truly memorable backdrop for castle weddings.

INNKEEPERS:	Donna and Jim Winner
ADDRESS:	422 East State Street
	Sharon, Pennsylvania 16146
TELEPHONE:	(724) 346-3046; (866) 345-2845
E-MAIL:	info@buhlmansion.com
WEBSITE:	www.buhlmansion.com
ROOMS:	10 Rooms; Private baths
CHILDREN:	Age 12 and older welcome
PETS:	Not allowed

Castle Coffee Cake

Makes 20 Servings

"...A quick and easy, yet delicious breakfast sweet."
~ Innkeeper, Buhl Mansion Guesthouse & Spa

Coffee Cake:
1	box Deluxe White Cake Mix
2	(16-ounce) cans apple pie filling
2	large eggs

Crumb Topping:
1	stick butter
2	cups brown sugar
2	tablespoons cinnamon
1½	cups flour

Preheat oven to 350°F. Combine cake mix, pie filling, and eggs in a large bowl. Beat at high speed for 2 minutes. Pour into greased 9x13-inch cake pan.

In a separate bowl, mix butter, brown sugar, cinnamon, and flour with a fork or pastry blender until crumb-like consistency.

Pour over cake batter. Make sweeping patterns with a knife until the crumb mixture is distributed evenly. Bake for 40 minutes.

Apple Bin Inn

APPLE BIN INN
● Bed & Breakfast ●

At the Apple Bin Inn, the proximity of the Amish neighbors provides a daily reminder to slow down and focus on the simpler things in life.

As you turn into the driveway, you'll be welcomed by an acre of park-like tranquility. Enter the main house as friends do, through the back door, and into the kitchen with an arched-brick hearth. The country dining room has the original wide-plank flooring and is the staging area for the scrumptious breakfast that will await you each morning. The comfortable living room features an extensive library to suit all reading tastes, along with comfy sofas and chairs for reading, knitting, games, or just talking with newfound friends. Once settled into a beautiful guest room, suite, or cottage, you'll know that the Apple Bin Inn combines the best of both worlds. Snuggle up under an antique family heirloom quilt and check the e-mail messages on your laptop computer using the inn's free wireless Internet access. During the summer months, the in-ground swimming pool will beckon you to take time to refresh and re-energize.

INNKEEPERS:	Steve and Jamie Shane
ADDRESS:	2835 Willow Street Pike
	Willow Street, Pennsylvania (Lancaster County) 17584
TELEPHONE:	(717) 464-5881; (800) 338-4296
E-MAIL:	stay@applebininn.com
WEBSITE:	www.applebininn.com
ROOMS:	5 Rooms; 2 Suites; 1 Cottage; Private baths
CHILDREN:	Welcome
PETS:	Not allowed; Resident cats

Upside Down Apple Coffee Cake

Makes 6 to 10 Servings

Adapted from *Pillsbury's Make it Easy Cookbook*

*"This is a fun, sticky, and delicious addition to your morning feast –
always enjoyed by all!" ~ Innkeeper, Apple Bin Inn Bed & Breakfast*

1½	cups Rome apples, peeled and chopped
1	can refrigerated cinnamon rolls with icing
½	cup pecan halves
2	tablespoons butter, melted
⅓	cup brown sugar, packed
2	tablespoons corn syrup

Preheat oven to 350°F. Grease a 9-inch glass pie pan with cooking spray. Spread 1 cup of apples evenly in pan. Separate dough into 8 rolls. Cut 4 of the rolls into 4 pieces. Cut the other 4 rolls into 6 pieces. Put the rolls in a large bowl. Add pecans and remaining apples. In small bowl, mix melted butter, brown sugar, and corn syrup; add to dough mixture and toss gently to combine. Spoon the dough mixture over apples in pie pan.

Bake for 30-35 minutes, or until deep golden brown. Cool in pan for 5 minutes, then invert onto a serving platter. Remove lid from icing, and microwave icing on high for 8-10 seconds. Drizzle icing over warm coffee cake and serve.

Field & Pine

Stately pine trees stand guard around this Early American farmhouse. Old boxwoods line the front walkway and gardens. The Field and Pine dwelling dates back to 1790. It was originally built as a tavern called "Sign of the Indian King." The inn has seven fireplaces and wide-plank pine floors. Join your host and other guests for a complimentary beverage, and listen to the innkeepers' stories about local history, traditions, and customs.

This 80-acre working farm includes a barn constructed from local limestone, where the sheep are housed and the grain and hay are stored. Watching the sheep graze on the pasture hill, and leisurely walks through the fields are favorite pastimes at the Field & Pine Bed and Breakfast. Big Spring, a short one-mile hike from the inn, forms one of the most famous limestone fly-fishing streams in Pennsylvania.

INNKEEPERS:	Allan and Mary Ellen Williams
ADDRESS:	2155 Ritner Highway
	Shippensburg, Pennsylvania 17257
TELEPHONE:	(717) 776-7179
E-MAIL:	fieldpine@kuhncom.net
WEBSITE:	www.bedandbreakfast.com/pennsylvania
ROOMS:	3 Rooms; 1 Suite; 2 Shared baths
CHILDREN:	Age 12 and older welcome
PETS:	Not allowed; Resident cat

Luscious Cranberry Coffee Cake

Makes 10 Servings

"This cake always brings raves and requests for the recipe. This cake can be baked, frozen, and served later." ~ Innkeeper, Field and Pine Bed & Breakfast

1	cup sugar
½	cup softened butter or margarine
2	eggs
½	teaspoon baking powder
1	teaspoon baking soda
½	teaspoon salt
2	cups flour
1	cup sour cream
1	teaspoon almond flavoring
1	(16-ounce) can whole berry cranberry sauce
½	cup walnuts or pecans, chopped

For the glaze:

¾	cup powdered sugar
2	tablespoons warm water
½	teaspoon almond flavoring

Preheat oven to 350°F. Cream the sugar and butter. Add eggs, baking powder, baking soda, and salt. Beat well. Alternately add the flour and sour cream to the sugar mixture, beginning and ending with the flour. Mix in almond flavoring. Pour ⅓ of the batter into a greased and floured, 10-inch tube pan. Add ½ can of cranberry sauce. Add next ⅓ of the batter, the other ½ can of cranberry sauce, and top with the last third of the batter. Sprinkle chopped nuts on top and bake for 1 hour. Cool for 5 minutes in the pan.

For the glaze: Combine all glaze ingredients.

Pour glaze over cake. Cool before removing from the pan.

Creekside Inn

Two stone tablets in the wall of the Creekside Inn Bed and Breakfast read, "Bilt by David and Esther Witmer" and "In the year of our Lord 1781." This eighteenth-century Georgian limestone home will welcome you as it did George Washington over 200 years ago. Built on 2 acres, the Creekside Inn property is part of an original William Penn land grant, peacefully situated along the Pequea Creek in the village of Paradise.

The Mennonite Church built its first meetinghouse in 1806 on land contributed by David Witmer, the village innkeeper, who was a member of the Mennonite congregation. The church tolerated the fact that David Witmer was an innkeeper, but several years after the church had been built, he was excommunicated because he used a carriage with "springs."

INNKEEPERS:	Cathy and Dennis Zimmermann
ADDRESS:	44 Leacock Road
	Paradise, Pennsylvania 17562
TELEPHONE:	(717) 687-0333; (866) 604-2574
E-MAIL:	cathy@thecreeksideinn.com
WEBSITE:	www.thecreeksideinn.com
ROOMS:	4 Rooms; 1 Suite; Private baths
CHILDREN:	Unable to accommodate
PETS:	Not allowed

Pumpkin Apple Streusel Cake

Makes 12 Servings

"Our guests love this cake. It is our most requested recipe."
~ Innkeeper, Creekside Inn Bed & Breakfast

2½	cups flour
2	cups sugar
1½	teaspoon cinnamon
1	teaspoon nutmeg
¼	teaspoon ginger
¼	teaspoon ground cloves
1	teaspoon baking soda
½	teaspoon salt
2	eggs
1	cup pumpkin puree
½	cup vegetable oil
2	cups apples, peeled and chopped

Topping:

2	tablespoons flour
¼	cup sugar
½	teaspoon cinnamon
4	teaspoons cold butter

Preheat oven to 350°F. In a large bowl, combine first 8 ingredients. In a medium bowl, combine eggs, pumpkin, and oil. Add liquid ingredients to the dry ingredients and stir until moist. Stir in apples. Pour into a greased 13x9-inch pan. Prepare streusel topping by mixing flour, sugar, and cinnamon. Cut in the cold butter. Sprinkle over the batter.

Bake for 35-40 minutes.

Reynolds Mansion

Linn Street
Bellefonte, Pennsylvania

As you pass through the iron gates, the 1885 Reynolds Mansion reveals its blend of Gothic, Italianate, and Queen Anne styles of architecture.

Enter the grand foyer and you'll see Eastlake woodwork, stained-glass windows, a brass candelabra, and a fireplace. The Victorians always did want to make a good first impression. The main staircase is hand-carved walnut with an ornate newel post and gas lamp. Three stained-glass windows illuminate the rich architectural details along the way. Grace's Garden Room was featured on the cover of *Country Victorian* magazine, showing its inlaid wood floor and sitting area in the turret. A ceiling mural of cherubs is the highlight of Louisa's Cherub Room. A full breakfast is served at the civilized hour of 9:00 A.M. Afterwards, take your coffee to the Snuggery and peruse the morning newspaper.

INNKEEPERS:	Joseph P. Heidt III, Joseph P. Heidt, Jr., and Charlotte Heidt
ADDRESS:	101 W. Linn Street
	Bellefonte, Pennsylvania 16823
TELEPHONE:	(814) 353-8407; (800) 899-3929
E-MAIL:	innkeeper@reynoldsmansion.com
WEBSITE:	www.reynoldsmansion.com
ROOMS:	6 Rooms; Private baths
CHILDREN:	Age 12 and older welcome
PETS:	Call ahead; Resident dogs and cat

Breakfast Cobbler

Makes 4 Servings

*"This is beautiful served on a plate with a doily flanked
on each side and cantaloupe slices for the garnish."*
~ Innkeeper, Reynolds Mansion Bed & Breakfast

$1\frac{1}{2}$	**tablespoons butter, softened**
$\frac{1}{2}$	**cup sugar**
2	**cups cranberries and blueberries, mixed**
2	**cups prepared pancake batter**
1	**teaspoon vanilla extract**
4	**ounces mascarpone cheese**
$\frac{1}{4}$	**cup maple syrup**

Preheat oven to 350°F. Butter bottom and inside of ramekins. Pour sugar into a ramekin and rotate until evenly coated. Pour excess sugar into next ramekin and repeat process; reserve remaining sugar. Pour $\frac{1}{2}$ cup of mixed berries into each ramekin. Combine pancake batter and vanilla. Pour $\frac{1}{2}$ cup of the mixture over fruit and sprinkle with sugar.

Place ramekins on center rack and bake for 25-30 minutes or until centers are firm and tops lightly browned.

Mix mascarpone cheese with maple syrup. When cobblers are baked, remove from oven and top each with a dollop of mascarpone/syrup mixture.

Homestead Lodging

A midst the freshness of well-kept fields, Homestead Lodging was built as a residence and bed and breakfast in 1984. Many guests have visited the inn multiple times over the years, and are known to the innkeepers by name. Bob and Lori Kepiro graciously share their knowledge of Lancaster County and the unique Amish culture of the area. Offering personal attention to the needs of their guests extends beyond the provision of fluffy towels and pillows. In the words of one guest, "the hospitality was as warm as the fire."

"It was first class all the way: immaculate and comfortable room; looking out the back window to see an Amish woman carrying her baby; the 'daily bread' in the room; yummy pastries... I'll be back soon! ~Guest

INNKEEPERS:	Bob and Lori Kepiro
ADDRESS:	184 Eastbrook Road, Route 896
	Smoketown, Pennsylvania 17576
TELEPHONE:	(717) 393-6927
E-MAIL:	LKepiro@comcast.net
WEBSITE:	www.homesteadlodging.net
ROOMS:	5 Rooms; Private baths
CHILDREN:	Welcome
PETS:	Not allowed

Country Apple Coffee Cake

Makes 6 Servings

"This recipe is okay to prepare the day ahead and then bake in the morning."
~ Innkeeper, Homestead Lodging Bed & Breakfast

2	tablespoons margarine or butter, softened
$1\frac{1}{2}$	cups apples; chopped, peeled and divided
1	(10-ounce) can Hungry Jack biscuits
$\frac{1}{3}$	cup brown sugar
$\frac{1}{4}$	teaspoon cinnamon
$\frac{1}{3}$	cup light corn syrup
1	egg
$\frac{1}{2}$	cup pecan halves or pieces

Glaze:

$\frac{1}{3}$	cup powdered sugar
$\frac{1}{4}$	teaspoon vanilla
1-2	teaspoons milk

Preheat oven to 350°F. Using 1 tablespoon of margarine, generously grease the bottom and sides of a 9-inch round or 8-inch square pan. Spread 1 cup of the apples in pan. Separate biscuit dough into 10 biscuits; quarter each biscuit. Arrange biscuit pieces point side up over apples. Top with remaining apples. In a small bowl, combine remaining tablespoon margarine, brown sugar, cinnamon, corn syrup, and egg; beat 2-3 minutes until sugar is partially dissolved. Stir in pecans. Spread over biscuit pieces.

Bake for 35-45 minutes. Mix powdered sugar, vanilla, and milk for glaze. Cool for 5 minutes. Drizzle glaze over the cake.

Macadamia Apricot Coffee Cake

Makes 8 Servings

"This is probably our guest's favorite breakfast treat."
~ Innkeeper, Homestead Lodging Bed & Breakfast

¾	cup macadamia nuts, chopped and divided
¼	cup sugar
1	tablespoon flour
2	tablespoons margarine, softened
1	egg, separated
1	8-ounce package crescent rolls
¼	cup apricot preserves
½	teaspoon orange zest

Topping:

5	teaspoons sugar
1	tablespoon flour
2	teaspoons margarine, softened

Preheat oven to 375°F. In small bowl, combine ½ cup of the chopped macadamia nuts, sugar, flour, margarine, and egg yolk. Mix well. Set aside. Unroll crescent dough into 2 long rectangles on ungreased cookie sheet, pressing seams together. Spread prepared filling lengthwise down center ⅓ of rectangle. In a small bowl, combine preserves and orange zest; spread over filling. Make diagonal cuts, 2 inches apart, on each side of the rectangle just to within 1/4 inch of filling. To give braided appearance, fold strips of dough at an angle across filling, alternating from side to side. Fold ends of coffee cake under to seal. Beat egg white slightly, brush over coffee cake.

For the topping: In small bowl, combine 5 teaspoons sugar, 1 tablespoon flour, 2 teaspoons margarine, and remaining nuts. Mix until consistency is crumbly. Sprinkle crumbs evenly over coffee cake.

Bake for 15 minutes.

Caramel Bubble Ring

Makes 10 to 12 Servings

¾	cup sugar
4	teaspoons cinnamon
2	packages (12-16) refrigerated breadsticks
⅓	cup margarine or butter, melted
⅓	cup pecans
½	cup caramel ice cream topping
2	tablespoons maple flavoring syrup

Preheat oven to 350°F. Combine the sugar and cinnamon; set aside. Separate each package of dough into 6 or 8 pieces. DO NOT UNROLL. Cut rolled pieces in half crosswise. Dip each piece of dough into melted margarine or butter. Roll in sugar and cinnamon mixture.

Generously grease a 10-inch fluted tube pan or bundt pan. Sprinkle about ½ of the pecans in bottom of pan. Arrange dough pieces, spiral side down, in the pan. Sprinkle with remaining pecans.

Combine caramel topping and maple flavoring syrup and stir. Drizzle over dough in pan. Bake for about 30 minutes or until dough is light brown. Cover with foil to prevent over browning, and bake for 10 more minutes.

Let stand 1 minute only. Invert onto a serving plate. Spoon any topping and nuts remaining in pan onto the ring. Serve warm.

The Filbert

"Life is grand at the Filbert"

The Filbert may well be the most supremely well-located bed and breakfast in northeast Pennsylvania. Located between the Lehigh Valley and the Pocono Mountains, it is a short distance from Philadelphia, Maryland, New York, and New Jersey. Yet, The Filbert is far removed from the chaos and clamor of the big cities. This well-restored ornate Victorian boasts a 60-foot-long porch complete with large, original fretwork. Many of the 200-year-old interior architectural details remain intact. The original wallpaper, dating to the late 1800s, continues to grace the walls.

The on-site general store, established in 1882, retains its original pressed-tin ceiling, wooden store counters, dry bins, and shelving. Pampering is also available on the premises: massage, skin, and nail care services may be reserved for your guaranteed relaxation.

INNKEEPERS:	Kathy and Terry Silfies
ADDRESS:	3740 Filbert Drive
	Danielsville, Pennsylvania 18038
TELEPHONE:	(610) 428-3300
E-MAIL:	filbertbnb@aol.com
WEBSITE:	www.filbertbnb.com
ROOMS:	4 Suites; 1 Family Suite; Private baths
CHILDREN:	Welcome
PETS:	Not allowed

Cheese Danish

Makes 16 Servings

"This is a quick and easy sweet treat to begin your breakfast."
~ Innkeeper, Filbert Bed & Breakfast

2	(8-ounce) packages cream cheese
1	egg yolk
1	cup sugar
1	teaspoon vanilla
2	(8-count) packages Pillsbury Crescent Rolls

Glaze: (optional)

2	tablespoons light corn syrup
2	tablespoons cornstarch
¾	cup sugar
1	cup water
3	tablespoons strawberry Jell-O

Preheat oven to 350°F. Mix cream cheese, egg yolk, sugar, and vanilla. Put a spoonful of cream cheese mixture in each triangle crescent. Do not roll into a crescent. Place on baking sheet and bake for 10 minutes.

For the glaze: Mix corn syrup, cornstarch, sugar, and water. Bring to a boil, stirring constantly until mixture becomes clear and thick. Remove from heat. Stir in Jell-O allowing it to thicken. Top crescents with glaze and serve.

The Lafayette Inn

Easton, Pennsylvania is the site of the July 8, 1776 reading of the Declaration of Independence. Easton is also home to the College Hill Historic District, a remarkable neighborhood where The Lafayette Inn is located in an 1895 Georgian mansion. The parlor boasts a grand piano and complementary tasting of cheeses and beverages from 4:00 until 6:00 on Friday and Saturday evenings.

The Lafayette Inn is a great central base from which to visit a number of interesting attractions. You can ride a steam train along the Delaware River; Lost River Caverns will satisfy your desire for spelunking; and Mule Drawn Canal Boat Rides on the Lehigh River will complement your tour of the National Canal Museum.

The Crayola Factory tour provides live demonstrations on how Crayola crayons and markers are made. And, Crayola has more than a dozen hands-on art activities for you to create a take-along memory of your visit.

INNKEEPERS:	Paul and Laura Di Liello
ADDRESS:	525 West Monroe Street
	Easton, Pennsylvania 18042
TELEPHONE:	(610) 253-4500; (800) 509-6990
E-MAIL:	info@lafayetteinn.com
WEBSITE:	www.lafayetteinn.com
ROOMS:	14 Rooms; 4 Suites; Private baths
CHILDREN:	Welcome
PETS:	Cats & dogs welcome in certain rooms

Homemade Granola

Makes 8 Servings

"Guests can't get enough of this delicious, crunchy treat. Enjoy with milk, yogurt or fruit, or eat it straight from the bag as a tasty snack." ~ Innkeeper, Lafayette Inn

1/3	cup honey
1/4	cup apple juice
1/2	cup chunky peanut butter
1/4	teaspoon vanilla extract
1/4	teaspoon ground cinnamon
3	cups old-fashioned rolled oats
1/2	cup wheat germ
1/2	cup almonds, chopped
1/2	cup pecans, chopped
1/2	cup walnuts, chopped
1/2	cup unsalted, raw sunflower seeds

Preheat oven to 300°F. In a saucepan over low heat, combine honey, apple juice, peanut butter, vanilla, and cinnamon. In a large bowl, combine oats, wheat germ, almonds, pecans, walnuts, and sunflower seeds. Pour honey mixture over oat mixture, and stir to coat. Spread granola on an ungreased baking sheet.

Bake for 20 minutes. Remove from oven, stir to break up; cool on baking sheet. Place in an air-tight container to store.

The Brafferton Inn

Filled with a mix of history, culture, and art, The Brafferton is the oldest continual residence in Gettysburg. Built in 1786, using brown stone native to the area, the three historic homes that comprise the Brafferton Inn are in the center of town, one-half block from Lincoln Square.

In July of 1863, the town of Gettysburg exploded in civil conflict. As Union troops passed the stone house on York Street, a Confederate sniper's bullet shattered the glass in an upstairs window and lodged in the mantel above the fireplace, where it remains today. For months after the battle, the house served as a Catholic chapel since the church was filled with wounded soldiers. The Brafferton Inn remains a sanctuary to this day.

A mural, encompassing all four walls in the dining room, is a conversational springboard for guests during breakfast at The Brafferton. Virginia Jacobs Mclaughlin, nationally recognized American primitive folk artist, painted this visual history lesson.

INNKEEPERS:	Joan, Brian, and Amybeth Hodges
ADDRESS:	44 York Street
	Gettysburg, Pennsylvania 17325
TELEPHONE:	(717) 337-3423; (866) 337-3423
E-MAIL:	innkeepers@brafferton.com
WEBSITE:	www.brafferton.com
ROOMS:	18 Rooms; 6 Suites; Private baths
CHILDREN:	Age 10 and older welcome
PETS:	Not allowed

Orange Roll

Makes 8 Servings

1	(8-count) can Pillsbury Grands Flaky Layer Biscuits

Filling:

8	teaspoons butter
9	teaspoons orange marmalade
10	teaspoons brown sugar

Icing:

1½	cups powdered sugar
¼	cup orange juice
1	teaspoon butter, softened
2	tablespoons cream cheese, softened
1	teaspoon orange zest

Preheat oven to 350°F. Grease cookie sheet with cooking spray. Roll out each biscuit to a 4-inch round. Layer 1 teaspoon of butter, marmalade, and brown sugar on each biscuit. Roll up each biscuit and place on cookie sheet, seam side down. Bake 8-10 minutes or until golden brown. Cool 5 minutes.

For the icing: Mix powdered sugar, orange juice, butter, cream cheese, and orange zest to the desired consistency for frosting.
Frost the rolls, and serve warm.

Sayre Mansion Inn

S ayre Mansion is the Lehigh Valley's premier urban inn. Located in the heart of Bethlehem's Fountain Hill Historic District, the mansion was originally the home of town icon and entrepreneur, Robert Sayre. One of eighteen guest rooms, the fabulous Conservatory Room, offers a 180-degree bird's-eye-view of Bethlehem. Spanning the full depth of the house, this rooftop refuge may be the most unique room in the house. But also comparable is the Library Room, featuring a large bedroom and separate sitting room/library with the original vaulted ceiling and chandelier. This literary haven contains two floor-to-ceiling bookcases and a gas fireplace surrounded in marble.

To start your day off right, help yourself to the breakfast buffet of fresh fruit, home-baked muffins, breads, and pastries. The Sayre Mansion offers a selection of hot breakfast entrees. Fresh-squeezed orange juice and rich-roasted coffee complement the delightful morning fare.

INNKEEPERS:	Carrie Ohlandt
ADDRESS:	250 Wyandotte Street
	Bethlehem, Pennsylvania 18015
TELEPHONE:	(610) 882-2100; (877) 345-9019
E-MAIL:	innkeeper@sayremansion.com
WEBSITE:	www.sayremansion.com
ROOMS:	18 Rooms
CHILDREN:	Welcome
PETS:	Welcome in one room

Rustic Grains

Makes 10 Servings

1	cup steel cut oats
2	cups rolled oats
¼	cup wheat berries
¼	cup barley
½	teaspoon salt
4	cups hot water
4	cups milk

Soak dry ingredients overnight in the hot water. Cook the next morning in milk for 1 hour at a simmer. Stir frequently. Add more salt, if desired. Thin with additional milk, if necessary. Leftovers may be reheated and will keep for three days, if refrigerated.

Mottern's B&B

Hummelstown is an old-fashioned community first settled by the Pennsylvania Dutch in the 1700s. Mottern's Bed and Breakfast is right in the center of town—an 1860s home with old house charm, and modernized for the twenty-first century. The bed and breakfast is a private suite of five rooms on the first floor, adjacent to a pergola-covered patio, which faces a walled and beautifully landscaped garden. A complimentary Hershey tour is included in your stay.

"Being only 2.5 miles from Hersheypark, we accommodate my 'chocoholics.' My favorite was being rewarded for winning a bet. Her husband had bet her she could not give up chocolate for one year. She won the bet and was rewarded with a trip to Hershey. She jokingly mentioned to me she had told him even the eggs were chocolate here. So, I had the local candy store make up chocolate 'dippy eggs' and their first morning served them with toast for breakfast. The look on both their faces was priceless!" ~Innkeeper

INNKEEPER:	Susan and Jeffrey Mottern
ADDRESS:	28 East Main Street
	Hummelstown, Pennsylvania 17036
TELEPHONE:	(717)566-3840
E-MAIL:	motternsbb@hotmail.com
WEBSITE:	www.motternsbb.com
ROOMS:	1 Room; 1 Suite; Private baths
CHILDREN:	Welcome
PETS:	Not allowed; Resident dogs

Oatmeal Crème Brûlée

Makes 8 Servings

"This is great for cold winter mornings."
~ Innkeeper, Mottern's Bed & Breakfast

2	**cups quick oats or 2½ cups old fashioned oats**
⅓	**cup sugar**
¼	**teaspoon salt (optional)**
3⅓	**cups milk or half & half**
2	**eggs or ½ cup egg substitute**
2	**teaspoons vanilla**
⅓	**cup brown sugar, firmly packed**

Preheat oven to 350°F. Combine oats, sugar, and salt in a medium bowl. Whisk milk, eggs, and vanilla in a separate bowl. Combine dry and wet ingredients and pour into greased baking dish. Bake for 40 minutes; center will jiggle slightly.

Remove from oven. Sprinkle evenly with brown sugar. With back of spoon, gently spread sugar in a thin layer across entire surface. Return to oven and bake 2-3 minutes until sugar melts.

Set oven to broil, and broil 3 inches from heat until sugar bubbles; 1-2 minutes. Watch carefully to prevent burning. Spoon into bowls and serve.

French Toast, Pancakes, & Waffles

French Toast,

Pancakes,

& Waffles

Terra Nova House

Innkeepers Barry and Sandy Miller were both born and raised in Easton. When their second careers ended, they began the search for their first bed and breakfast. They discovered their perfect 1901 Victorian in Mercer County's Grove City, and called it Terra Nova House. The other permanent residents of the home are: Jada, a precocious Silver Back Persian, who will tug at your heartstrings with a single look; and Molly, the lovable Golden Retriever who will always want to give you her favorite toy. A hand-painted ocean mural graces the walls of the Caribbean Room, one of five guestrooms. The British Empire Room's deep red tones capture the flavor of English royalty. Tasty home-cooked breakfasts are presented in the airy and intimate dining room. China cupboards and a corner fireplace complete the cozy feel of this room.

INNKEEPERS:	Barry and Sandy Miller
ADDRESS:	322 West Poplar Street
	Grove City, Pennsylvania 16127
TELEPHONE:	(724) 450-0712; (877) 837-6682
E-MAIL:	info@terranovahouse.com
WEBSITE:	www.terranovahouse.com
ROOMS:	4 Rooms; 1 Suites; Private baths
CHILDREN:	Age 12 and older welcome
PETS:	Not allowed

Cranberry Bog French Toast

Makes 8 Servings

1	cup brown sugar
½	cup butter, melted
3	teaspoons cinnamon, divided
½	cup dried cranberries
4	tart apples, peeled and sliced
1	loaf French or Italian bread
6	eggs
1½	cups milk
1	tablespoon vanilla extract

Combine brown sugar, butter, and 1 teaspoon cinnamon in a bowl. Pour into a 9x13-inch baking dish. Add cranberries and peeled, sliced apples to baking dish. Toss to coat apples and cranberries well.

Cut bread into 1-inch slices. Arrange bread on top of mixture in baking dish.

In a separate bowl, mix eggs, milk, vanilla, and remaining 2 teaspoons of cinnamon. Pour over mixture in baking dish; soaking bread completely.

Cover and refrigerate overnight.

Preheat oven to 375°F. Cover with foil and bake for 40 minutes. Uncover and bake 5 more minutes. Let stand 5 minutes. Serve inverted on plate.

The Brafferton Inn

Filled with a mix of history, culture, and art, The Brafferton is the oldest continual residence in Gettysburg. Built in 1786, using brown stone native to the area, the three historic homes that comprise the Brafferton Inn are in the center of town, one-half block from Lincoln Square.

In July of 1863, the town of Gettysburg exploded in civil conflict. As Union troops passed the stone house on York Street, a Confederate sniper's bullet shattered the glass in an upstairs window and lodged in the mantel above the fireplace, where it remains today. For months after the battle, the house served as a Catholic chapel since the church was filled with wounded soldiers. The Brafferton Inn remains a sanctuary to this day.

A mural, encompassing all four walls in the dining room, is a conversational springboard for guests during breakfast at The Brafferton. Virginia Jacobs Mclaughlin, nationally recognized American primitive folk artist, painted this visual history lesson.

INNKEEPERS:	Joan, Brian, and Amybeth Hodges
ADDRESS:	44 York Street
	Gettysburg, Pennsylvania 17325
TELEPHONE:	(717) 337-3423; (866) 337-3423
E-MAIL:	innkeepers@brafferton.com
WEBSITE:	www.brafferton.com
ROOMS:	18 Rooms; 6 Suites; Private baths
CHILDREN:	Age 10 and older welcome
PETS:	Not allowed

Raspberry Croissant French Toast

Makes 4 Servings

1	cup half & half
2	eggs
¼	cup sugar
1	teaspoon cinnamon
4	croissants
8	tablespoons of raspberry preserves
1	teaspoon butter, melted
1	pint of fresh raspberries, for garnish

Whipped cream, for garnish
Maple syrup, on the side

Combine half & half, eggs, sugar, and cinnamon in 9x13-inch baking dish. Cut croissants in half horizontally and spread 2 tablespoons of preserves on each of 4 of the croissant halves. Top with the 4 remaining halves and press together. Place croissants in egg mixture; turning to coat. Let soak for 30 minutes.

Heat griddle or large skillet over medium high heat; coat with 1 teaspoon of melted butter. Slowly brown croissants, about 4 minutes on each side. Place on a plate and garnish with fresh raspberries and whipped cream. Serve with maple syrup on the side.

The Mercersburg Inn

Plush feather beds and Egyptian cotton linens are standard amenities in the seventeen divine guestrooms at The Mercersburg Inn. A magnificent view of the Tuscarora Mountain can be seen from the Dressing Room. French doors in the room lead to a small, private balcony under the inn's portico. The multi-paned window adds architectural flair to the additional loft bedroom in The Loft suite. There is a carriage house, built in 1909, behind the turn-of-the-century Georgian mansion. Its newly constructed upper floor houses two additional rooms.

The filling goat cheese torte and sweet strawberry pancakes are two of guest's breakfast favorites at The Mercersburg Inn. Byron's Dining Room Restaurant offers delectable evening meals. The inn offers French cooking classes on-site on weekends. You can cook with world-renowned chef Francois Dionot from the celebrated L'Academie de Cuisine.

INNKEEPERS:	Lisa and Jim McCoy
ADDRESS:	405 South Main Street
	Mercersburg, Pennsylvania 17236
TELEPHONE:	(717) 328-5231
E-MAIL:	lisa@mercersburginn.com
WEBSITE:	www.mercersburginn.com
ROOMS:	17 Rooms; Private Baths
CHILDREN:	Age 7 and older welcome
PETS:	Not allowed

French Bread Custard

Makes 8 Servings

1	loaf French bread
4	ounces unsalted butter; melted
4	whole eggs
2	egg yolks
$\frac{1}{2}$	cup sugar
$\frac{1}{4}$	teaspoon nutmeg
3	cups whole milk
1	cup heavy cream
1	teaspoon vanilla

Powdered sugar, fresh fruit, and maple syrup, for garnish

Remove crust from the French bread and cut into $1\frac{1}{2}$-inch slices. Brush both sides of the bread with melted butter. Arrange the bread in a 9x12-inch pan.

Beat the eggs and egg yolks, add sugar and nutmeg; whisk well to combine. Add milk, cream, and vanilla. Whisk well. Pour over bread.

Refrigerate overnight.

Preheat oven to 350°F. Place the pan of French bread custard in a larger pan filled half-full with hot water. Bake for 45 minutes or until lightly browned and puffy. Dust with powdered sugar, and garnish with fresh fruit and maple syrup.

Dillweed

Dillweed Bed and Breakfast is a turn-of-the-century home built by the Dill family, early settlers of Dilltown. Antique hats, hatpins, vintage clothing, and antique toys are all part of the decor in the four guestrooms and the Garden Suite. The rooms have the charming names of Parsley, Sage, Rosemary, and Thyme. The Parsley Room has a particularly good view of Dillweed's herb garden. The on-site Trailside Shop offers two floors of country gifts and antiques for your browsing pleasure.

Dillweed is located at the beginning of Ghost Town Trail, an historic rail-trail project. The limestone-surfaced trail passes by once-thriving mining communities, following Blacklick Creek. The Ghost Town Trail is a multi-use recreational trail appropriate for hiking, biking, horseback riding, and cross-country skiing.

INNKEEPERS:	Corey, Kyra and Cindy Gilmore
ADDRESS:	PO Box 1
	Dilltown, Pennsylvania 15929
TELEPHONE:	(814) 446-6465
E-MAIL:	dillweed@floodcity.net
WEBSITE:	www.dillweedinc.com
ROOMS:	4 Rooms; 1 Suite; Private and shared baths
CHILDREN:	Welcome
PETS:	Not allowed

French Toast Goes Dilly

Makes 6 Servings

"This is a savory breakfast entrée. Experiment with other herb combinations. Basil is a wonderful variation." ~ Innkeeper, Dillweed Bed & Breakfast

4	eggs
¼	cup sour cream
3	tablespoons freshly snipped dill weed
1	tablespoon Dijon mustard
1	tablespoon butter
6	slices French bread, ½-inch thick
1	tomato, cut into 6 thin slices
6	tablespoons cheddar cheese, grated
6	dill flowerets, for garnish

Combine first 4 ingredients and mix well. Melt butter on griddle. Dip bread into egg mixture; 10 seconds on each side. Grill lightly.

To serve: Top each slice with thinly sliced tomato. Sprinkle with 1 tablespoon Cheddar cheese. Melt under broiler. Garnish plate with dill floweret.

Furnace Hills

An expansive log home on eight wooded acres is the secluded retreat you'll discover at the Furnace Hills Bed and Breakfast in northern Lancaster County. The wood-burning stove enhances the ambiance in the Great Room. Peer out of the window and catch a glimpse of songbirds, whitetail deer, or one of the other furry or feathered residents. Downey woodpeckers are regular visitors to the suet feeder, and at night, flying squirrels often drop in. The hot tub on the deck is positioned perfectly for stargazing, bird watching, or even for seeing the sunrise.

If you are up for a hike, you can set out on a short loop trail through the mixed hardwood forest. Or, if you're a little more ambitious, you can take the horseshoe trail and hike 1.5 miles to the Middle Creek Wildlife Management Area.

Hearty, traditional, or Pennsylvania Dutch breakfasts are made to order. The English Muffins, sticky buns and jellies are all homemade.

INNKEEPERS:	Ben and Liz Ehrhart
ADDRESS:	575 Mountain Top Drive
	Denver, Pennsylvania 17517
TELEPHONE:	(717) 733-3897; (877) 477-3557
E-MAIL:	innkeeper@furnacehills.com
WEBSITE:	www.furnacehills.com
ROOMS:	4 Rooms; Private baths
CHILDREN:	Call ahead
PETS:	Not allowed; Resident dog

Caramel French Toast Baked

Makes 6 to 8 Servings

"Great recipe to use for overnight guests or special holidays
for family since you put it together the night before."
~ Innkeeper, Furnace Hills Bed & Breakfast

$1\frac{1}{2}$	cups brown sugar
1	cup butter, divided
$\frac{1}{4}$	cup corn syrup
10	slices French bread, $\frac{1}{2}$-inch thick
4	eggs, beaten
$2\frac{1}{2}$	cups milk
1	tablespoon vanilla
3	tablespoons sugar
$1\frac{1}{2}$	teaspoons cinnamon
$\frac{1}{4}$	cup butter, melted

In saucepan over medium heat, mix and stir the brown sugar, $\frac{3}{4}$ cup butter, and corn syrup until bubbly. Pour evenly into greased 9x13-inch baking dish. Arrange bread evenly over syrup. Combine eggs, milk, and vanilla. Stir well and pour over bread. Cover and chill at least 8 hours.

In the morning: preheat oven to 350°F. Combine sugar and cinnamon; sprinkle over bread. Drizzle $\frac{1}{4}$ cup melted butter over cinnamon/sugar.

Bake uncovered for 45 minutes.

The Inn at New Berlin

An uptown experience in rural central Pennsylvania, The Inn at New Berlin is in the center of an old German town. Pastoral Susquehanna Valley is the gentle backdrop for the 1906 Victorian Jacob Schoch House, and the 1838 Federal-style Samuel Aurand House. Both homes provide lodging for The Inn at New Berlin.

The morning glory for any overnight visit is the full breakfast, served daily at Gabriel's Restaurant. A celebrated bill of fare is also available for dinner at Gabriel's, served Wednesday through Sunday. Chef Scott Brouse is the self-taught culinary wizard behind the eclectic menus with Pennsylvania flourishes. Seasonal herbs and vegetables are fresh from the inn's gardens.

"A luxurious base for indulging in a clutch of quiet pleasures..."
~ The Philadelphia Inquirer

INNKEEPERS:	Robert and Nancy Schanck
ADDRESS:	321 Market Street
	New Berlin, Pennsylvania 17855
TELEPHONE:	(570) 966-0321; (800) 797-2350
E-MAIL:	stay@innatnewberlin.com
WEBSITE:	www.innatnewberlin.com
ROOMS:	9 Rooms; 2 Suites; Private baths
CHILDREN:	Age 8 and under welcome in 2 rooms
PETS:	Not allowed

Walnut & Cream Cheese Stuffed French Toast

Makes 7 Servings

14	slices Italian bread, 1-inch thick
1	tablespoon butter
1	cup apple, peeled and diced
½	tablespoon maple syrup
1	tablespoon brown sugar
½	teaspoon cinnamon
1	(8-ounce package) cream cheese, room temperature
½	cup walnuts, chopped

Egg Batter:

10	eggs
⅓	cup half & half
¼	cup sugar
1	tablespoon vanilla extract

Melt butter in a 10-inch sauté pan over medium heat. Add apples, maple syrup, brown sugar, and cinnamon. Cook until apples begin to turn golden brown, about 5-7 minutes. Remove and cool. Combine cream cheese, walnuts, and cooked apples.

Butterfly* the 1-inch slices of bread. Spread 2 tablespoons of cream cheese filling on one side of bread and close together. Repeat for the remaining slices.

For the egg batter: Whisk all of the ingredients in a medium sized bowl. Dip each stuffed bread slice into egg batter. Coat well and drain off excess. Brown French toast on a greased grill over medium heat, about 3 minutes per side.

Butterfly (definition taken from The New Food Lover's Companion)
To split a food down the center, cutting almost but not completely through.
The two halves are then opened flat to resemble a butterfly shape.

1811 *Addison House*

D eer are plentiful on the grounds surrounding Addison House, and the Choconut Creek meanders by the farm on its way to the Susquehanna. An occasional black bear ambles down from the mountains. Inside, the warmth of a roaring fire on a chilly day, and a wealth of good books in the library are awaiting Addison House guests. This room is especially cozy, with big leather lounge chairs accompanied by large, soft footstools.

Addison House has received the Historic Preservation Award for Outstanding Restoration. All accommodations are furnished with Victorian and Empire antiques. Afternoon teas are available.

Turndown service is offered with delicious chocolates, and chilled spring water served in an antique carafe. Amenity baskets overflowing with information on activities and tours in the Endless Mountains are located in each room.

INNKEEPERS:	Gloria and Dennis McLallen
ADDRESS:	Route 267 South
	Choconut, Pennsylvania 18818
TELEPHONE:	(570) 553-2682
E-MAIL:	gloria@1811addison.com
WEBSITE:	www.1811addison.com
ROOMS:	3 Rooms; 1 Suite; Private and shared baths
CHILDREN:	Age 4 and over welcome
PETS:	Not allowed; Resident cat

Creamy Peach Filled French Toast

Makes 6 to 8 Servings

Adapted from *Breakfasts and Brunches*

"I have been serving this recipe for 19 years. Guests who make return trips to stay at my B&B always ask for the peach French toast. I sometimes use chopped strawberries. I serve my French toast with powdered sugar." ~ Innkeeper, 1811 Addison House

3	**ounces cream cheese, softened**
$\frac{1}{2}$	**cup peaches, chopped**
2	**tablespoons pecans, chopped**
1	**tablespoon honey**
6-8	**slices French bread, cut diagonally, 1-$\frac{1}{2}$ inches thick**
2	**eggs**
$\frac{1}{2}$	**cup half & half**
$\frac{1}{4}$	**teaspoon vanilla**

Butter, sliced fresh fruit, and honey or maple syrup, for topping

In small bowl, beat cream cheese until light and fluffy. Add peaches, pecans, and honey; blend well. With a small knife, split the rounded top of each bread slice to form a pocket for the cheese mixture; carefully fill with 1$\frac{1}{2}$ tablespoons of the mixture.

In a shallow bowl or pie pan, slightly beat eggs. Add half & half and vanilla; mix well. Heat a large skillet or griddle. Lightly grease the heated skillet.

Being careful not to squeeze the filled slices, dip bread in egg mixture, turning to coat both sides. Cook in skillet over medium heat about 3-4 minutes on each side or until golden brown. Serve with butter, additional sliced fresh fruit, and honey or maple syrup.

American Vintage

A rare find indeed, American Vintage Bed and Breakfast is one of Southern York County's oldest farmhouses residing on a working farm. The four-story, 1780 home is constructed of fieldstones, with walls three to four feet thick. The structure of American Vintage causes one to reflect on the masterful carpenters of yesteryear who relied on the integration of natural material from the earth, and little but their hands with which to work. Inside, the chestnut and pine-plank walls add a rich flavor to the home.

From the farmlands, ducks, and friendly dogs to Granny's French Toast, guests rave about their tranquil experience at the American Vintage Bed and Breakfast. Here is a very special paraphrased poem sent to the Innkeeper from a couple who lives in Johannesburg, South Africa:

"Tis thy land and my land, the best of lands on earth, so cherish it my children, for it's yours by right of birth."

INNKEEPERS:	Jo Ann Dalton
ADDRESS:	5740 Thompson Road
	Stewartstown, Pennsylvania 17363
TELEPHONE:	(717) 993-9971; (866) 204-9995
E-MAIL:	vintagebandb@cs.com
WEBSITE:	www.americanvintagebandb.com
ROOMS:	4 Rooms; 1 Suite; 2 Private baths
CHILDREN:	Welcome
PETS:	Welcome; Resident dog

Pumpkin Toast Delight

Makes 8 Servings

"...A great breakfast for that chilly morning. I love it because I can prepare and bake the same day, or refrigerate overnight and bake the next morning."
~ Innkeeper, American Vintage Bed & Breakfast

1½	**cups light brown sugar**
1	**cup butter, melted**
1	**(16-ounce) can pure pumpkin**
Allspice, to taste	
6	**eggs**
1½	**teaspoons vanilla**
1½	**cups milk**
1	**loaf French bread, 1-inch slices**

Preheat oven to 325°F. Combine brown sugar and butter in a 9x13-inch cake pan; spreading evenly. Spread pumpkin evenly over the top of the sugar and butter. Sprinkle allspice over the pumpkin.

Combine eggs, vanilla, and milk in a medium size bowl; beat well.

Cut French bread into 1-inch slices and dip into egg mixture, letting the bread become saturated. Place bread on top of the pumpkin mixture.

Bake for 25 minutes.

The Parsonage

Constructed in 1844, The Parsonage is the oldest, unaltered building in the town of Jim Thorpe (formerly Mauch Chunk.) The house was built by the Reverend Richard Webster, pastor of the First Presbyterian Church of Mauch Chunk. The four-story, brick home was inhabited by Reverend Webster, his wife Elizabeth, and their seven children until their deaths.

The Mauch Chunk Room is one of the four bedrooms at The Parsonage. A stool is needed to climb into the dark mahogany, four-poster bed. A rubbing from a tombstone in England, detailing the marriage vows of two people in love, is hung over the bed. The cool tones of green and the warmth of chocolate brown in the Lehigh Room add to the calming effect this room has on your senses. Enjoy your full breakfast in the Tiffany bay-windowed dining room, and then relax and take a book to the screened gazebo that's situated in the lush gardens.

INNKEEPERS:	Maureen Grant
ADDRESS:	61 West Broadway
	Jim Thorpe, Pennsylvania 18229
TELEPHONE:	(570) 325-4462; (800) 799-0244
E-MAIL:	parsonagebb@yahoo.com
WEBSITE:	www.theparsonagebandb.com
ROOMS:	4 Rooms; Private baths
CHILDREN:	Age 15 and older welcome
PETS:	Not allowed; resident cat

Pumpkin Pancakes

Makes 18 Pancakes

2	cups biscuit mix (Bisquick works well)
2	tablespoons brown sugar
2	teaspoons ground cinnamon
2	eggs
1	(12-ounce) can evaporated milk
½	cup pumpkin, cooked or canned
2	tablespoons vegetable oil
1	teaspoon vanilla extract

Maple syrup, for topping

Combine biscuit mix, brown sugar, and cinnamon in a bowl; set aside.
In a separate bowl, combine eggs, milk, pumpkin, oil, and vanilla. Stir into dry ingredients and mix well.

Pour batter by ⅓ cupfuls onto a lightly greased hot griddle; turn when bubbles form on top of pancakes. Cook until both sides are golden brown. Serve with maple syrup.

Pheasant Field

The three-acre pond and island, along with ten acres of farmland, is the habitat for bullfrogs, geese, and songbirds to create a symphony on summer evenings at the Pheasant Field Bed and Breakfast. Your accommodations are provided in the 200-year-old central Pennsylvania brick farmhouse. The family room, once the summer kitchen, was used as a stop on the Underground Railroad.

An inviting dining room welcomes you for a country breakfast, served at your convenience from 5:30 to 10:30 A.M. on most mornings. On-site tennis courts at Pheasant Field offer the perfect opportunity for you to practice your backhand. During your visit you can stable your horse in the historic stone barn. Pastures and run-in sheds are also available. The Appalachian Trail is less than a mile away. Maps of hiking routes on the Trail, as well as menus from area restaurants, are conveniently on hand at the bed and breakfast.

INNKEEPERS:	Dee Segan and Chuck DeMarco
ADDRESS:	150 Hickorytown Road
	Carlisle, Pennsylvania 17013
TELEPHONE:	(717) 258-0717; (877) 258-0717
E-MAIL:	stay@pheasantfield.com
WEBSITE:	www.pheasantfield.com
ROOMS:	7 Rooms; 2 Suites; 1 Cottage; Private baths
CHILDREN:	Age 8 and older welcome
PETS:	Dogs, cats and horses welcome with limited availability

Oatmeal Pancakes

Makes 18 Pancakes

Adapted from *The Country Inn and Bed & Breakfast Cookbook Vol. 1.*

"Our guests just love these pancakes. Plan ahead. The batter needs to rest overnight." ~ Innkeeper, Pheasant Field Bed & Breakfast

2	**cups rolled oats**
2	**cups buttermilk**
2	**eggs, lightly beaten**
1/2	**stick butter, melted and cooled**
1/2	**cup raisins and/or chopped nuts (optional)**
1/2	**cup flour**
2	**tablespoons sugar**
1	**teaspoon baking soda**
1	**teaspoon baking powder**
1/2	**teaspoon cinnamon**
1/4	**teaspoon salt**

Syrup or jam, for topping

Combine oats and buttermilk in a medium bowl; stir to blend well. Cover and refrigerate until the next day.

Just before cooking, add eggs, butter, and raisins or nuts (if desired) to oat mixture; stir just to blend. In a small bowl, combine flour, sugar, baking soda, baking powder, cinnamon, and salt; add to oat mixture and stir just until moistened. (The batter will be thicker than regular pancakes; if the batter seems too thick, add up to 3 more tablespoons of buttermilk.) Preheat a griddle and grease lightly. Pour batter onto griddle. Cook until browned on each side. Serve with warm syrup or jam.

Keller House

The Keller family occupied this home in the farm country of Penn Valley for over ninety years. The Keller House was built in 1887, in the village of Centre Valley. Your hosts at the Keller House today, Ernie and Kathy Mowery, beckon travelers to join them in the sitting room to share the old-fashioned pleasure of the Edison Victrola.

Later in the evening, retire to the Romance Room with a private Jacuzzi for two. Or, choose the General's Hideaway with pictures of Civil War era generals adorning both bedroom and bathroom. Melt your cares away as you soak in the antique claw-foot bathtub in the Garden Suite.

Your morning fare will be presented on china and crystal, once used by the Keller family. A couple of The Keller House breakfast favorites are Ernie's Famous Sausage Peach Puff Pancakes, and the Egg'stra Special Breakfast Casserole.

INNKEEPERS:	Ernie and Kathy Mowery
ADDRESS:	109 West Church Street
	Centre Hall, Pennsylvania 16828
TELEPHONE:	(814) 364-2225; (888) 554-2588
E-MAIL:	info@kellerhousebb.com
WEBSITE:	www.kellerhousebb.com
ROOMS:	4 Rooms; 1 Suites; Private baths
CHILDREN:	Age 13 and older welcome
PETS:	Not allowed

Sausage Peach Puff Pancakes

Makes 2 to 4 Pancakes

"I usually cook the filling until the pancake is done, about 10-15 minutes. The pancake will rise in the oven, but it falls after you remove it. If a guest prefers not to eat meat, you may substitute any seasonal fruit for the sausage."
~ Innkeeper, Keller House Bed & Breakfast

Pancake:
½	cup flour
1	tablespoon sugar
⅛	teaspoon salt
2	eggs, beaten
½	cup milk
1	tablespoon margarine or butter

Filling:
8-10	pork sausage links
1	(16-ounce) can sliced peaches, drained
⅓	cup pancake syrup

Dash ground nutmeg

Preheat oven to 425°F. In a mixing bowl, combine flour, sugar, and salt; whisk in eggs and milk until smooth. Place butter in a 9-inch pie plate. Place in heated oven until butter melts. Pour batter onto the hot plate. Bake 10 to 15 minutes or until edges are golden brown.

In a skillet, cook the sausage until done; stir in peaches, syrup, and nutmeg. Bring to a boil. Reduce heat and simmer for 7-10 minutes. Pour onto pancake. Serve immediately.

The Brickhouse Inn

Gettysburg's historic downtown is well represented by the Brickhouse Inn, an 1898 three-story brick Victorian, along with the adjacent Welty House, built it 1830. The National Battlefield Park is virtually at your doorstep, and Lincoln Square in the town center is only a few minutes away. The area's shops are filled with Civil War collectibles.

The Brickhouse Inn was once the home of a local banker and his family. The historic Welty House, built by Solomon Welty, was in the thick of fighting during the Battle of Gettysburg. Its walls still bear the scars of bullets. Guest accommodations are named for the states represented in the battle at Gettysburg.

The breakfasts are plentiful and delicious. The menu changes daily, but the morning fare always includes the signature dish, Pennsylvania Dutch Shoo Fly Pie. Lemonade and homemade cookies are served in the afternoon.

INNKEEPERS:	Tessa Bardo, Brian Duncan, and Melanie Driscoll
ADDRESS:	452 Baltimore Street
	Gettysburg, Pennsylvania 17325
TELEPHONE:	(717) 338-9337; (800) 864-3464
E-MAIL:	stay@brickhouseinn.com
WEBSITE:	www.brickhouseinn.com
ROOMS:	13 Rooms; 2 Suites; Private baths
CHILDREN:	Age 10 and older welcome
PETS:	Not allowed

Apple Pancakes

Makes 4 to 5 Servings

Apple Mixture:

2	tablespoons butter
1	tablespoon brown sugar
$\frac{1}{2}$	cup golden raisins (optional)
2	small or 1 large Granny Smith apple(s); peeled, cored, and chopped
1	teaspoon cinnamon
$\frac{1}{4}$	teaspoon ginger

Batter:

2	cups Bisquick	2	tablespoons sugar
$1\frac{1}{4}$	cups milk	1	teaspoon vanilla
2	eggs	2	tablespoons oil

Apple Cinnamon Syrup:

$\frac{1}{2}$	cup sugar
1	tablespoon cornstarch
1	teaspoon cinnamon
1	tablespoon lemon juice
1	cup apple juice or apple cider
2	tablespoons butter

Preheat oven to 350°F. In a frying pan, melt butter and sauté raisins and apples with brown sugar, cinnamon, and ginger until cooked but firm, about 8 minutes. In large bowl, combine batter ingredients and mix until well blended. Grease sides and bottom (not rim) of a 9-inch pie plate. Pour the batter into the prepared pie plate. Spoon the apple mixture over the top of the batter. Bake 25-30 minutes or until knife inserted in the center comes out clean.

Syrup:
In a saucepan, stir sugar, cornstarch, and cinnamon until blended. Add lemon juice and apple juice or apple cider. Bring to a boil over medium heat, stirring often. When the syrup boils, reduce heat to simmer and add butter. Simmer until butter is melted, stirring occasionally. Drizzle over pancake and serve.

Morgan Century Farm

Established in 1850 as a family farm, the original farmhouse, one barn, and two outbuildings still remain on the Morgan Century Farm grounds. A small milk house built in the 1930s now serves as a potting shed. In 1995, great-great granddaughter, Linda Faye Morgan, and her husband Ken Florentine began a three-year restoration of the main building as a country inn. Being antique car lovers, with a special interest in Plymouths, Ken and Linda named each guest room in the main house after a Plymouth model of the early 1950s. A rustic two-story cottage, meant just for two, is another lodging choice at Morgan Century Farm. Or, you may want to consider the old barn hayloft with its deck extending out above Elks Creek. The Elegant Duck Gift Shop is located in the lower part of the barn.

Each morning, a three-course breakfast is served, with complimentary wine and cheese offered in the afternoon.

INNKEEPERS:	Ken and Linda Florentine
ADDRESS:	Route 1 Lincoln Falls
	Forksville, Pennsylvania 18616
TELEPHONE:	(570) 924-4909; (888) 335-1583
E-MAIL:	morcenfm@epix.net
WEBSITE:	www.pa-bedandbreakfast.com
ROOMS:	5 Rooms; 1 Cottage; Private baths
CHILDREN:	Unable to accommodate
PETS:	Welcome in the cottage; Resident cat

Iron Skillet Pancakes

Makes 4 to 6 Servings

"This is a very easy breakfast treat."
~ Innkeeper, Morgan Century Farm Bed & Breakfast

1	**cup flour**
½	**teaspoon salt**
4	**large eggs**
1	**cup milk**
4	**tablespoons butter or ½ stick unsalted butter**

Powdered sugar, maple syrup, or apple butter, for topping

Preheat oven to 450°F. In a medium bowl, sift the flour and salt. In a separate bowl, whisk the eggs and milk. Add the egg mixture to the dry ingredients; stir until just blended.

In 12-inch iron skillet, melt butter until hot and frothy. Pour batter into skillet and transfer quickly to the oven. Bake for 20-25 minutes. Be sure not to open the oven while baking. Serve with powdered sugar, maple syrup, or apple butter.

The Mercersburg Inn

Plush feather beds and Egyptian cotton linens are standard amenities in the seventeen divine guestrooms at The Mercersburg Inn. A magnificent view of the Tuscarora Mountain can be seen from the Dressing Room. French doors in the room lead to a small, private balcony under the inn's portico.

The multi-paned window adds architectural flair to the additional loft bedroom in The Loft suite. There is a carriage house, built in 1909, behind the turn-of-the-century Georgian mansion. Its newly constructed upper floor houses two additional rooms.

The filling goat cheese torte and sweet strawberry pancakes are two of guest's breakfast favorites at The Mercersburg Inn. Byron's Dining Room Restaurant offers delectable evening meals. The inn offers French cooking classes on-site on weekends. You can cook with world-renowned chef Francois Dionot from the celebrated L'Academie de Cuisine.

INNKEEPERS:	Lisa and Jim McCoy
ADDRESS:	405 South Main Street
	Mercersburg, Pennsylvania 17236
TELEPHONE:	(717) 328-5231
E-MAIL:	lisa@mercersburginn.com
WEBSITE:	www.mercersburginn.com
ROOMS:	17 Rooms; Private Baths
CHILDREN:	Age 7 and older welcome
PETS:	Not allowed

Sour Cream Waffles

Makes 4 to 6 Waffles

"These waffles will melt in your mouth." ~ Innkeeper, Mercersburg Inn

1	cup flour, sifted 5 times
1	teaspoon baking powder
⅛	teaspoon salt
1½	teaspoons sugar
1	teaspoon baking soda
3	eggs, separated
2	cups sour cream
3	tablespoons butter, melted

Cooking spray
Garnish, of your choice

Combine flour, baking powder, salt, sugar, and baking soda in a large bowl; sift.

In a medium bowl, beat egg yolks; add sour cream and melted butter. Stir the yolk mixture into the dry ingredients as quickly as possible. In a medium bowl, beat the egg whites until stiff peaks form. Fold egg whites lightly and carefully into batter. Spray waffle iron with cooking spray and heat on high. Pour approximately 1 cup of the batter into waffle iron.

Bake 2½-3 minutes. Serve garnished, as desired.

Jackson House

The only bed and breakfast located on the Heritage Rail Trail is The Jackson House, built in 1859 in the quaint little town of Railroad, in southern York County. The stone cistern that stored the hotel's water supply in days long past is still intact today, as is the original dumbwaiter that was once used for service in the old hotel. The Jackson House Great Room has antique furnishings that have enough character to tell their own tales. A gorgeously landscaped hillside, terraced gardens, several ponds and fountains, and a waterfall encourage time spent outdoors.

On Friday and Saturday evenings, all summer long, the Naylor Winery offers reasonably priced concerts for a variety of musical tastes. Just six miles up the road from The Jackson House, concerts are held rain or shine. They have a large covered pavilion with a dance floor. Naylor Winery sells bottles of their own wine on-site, and they will even open it for you.

INNKEEPERS:	Jean and George Becker
ADDRESS:	6 East Main Street
	Railroad, Pennsylvania 17355
TELEPHONE:	(717) 227 2022; (877) STA-IN-PA
E-MAIL:	JacksonHouseBnB@JacksonHouseBandB.com
WEBSITE:	www.JacksonHouseBandB.com
ROOMS:	2 Rooms; 2 Suites; 1 cottage; private baths
CHILDREN:	Age 12 and older welcome
PETS:	Small pets welcome in the Wille G. Suite; call ahead; Resident dog

Blueberry Waffles

Makes 6 Waffles

*"Guests say these are the best waffles they have ever had.
They're light, fluffy, and what a wonderful presentation.
This batter needs to be refrigerated overnight."*
~ Innkeeper, Jackson House Bed & Breakfast

3	cups Bisquick
1¾	cups whole milk
1	tablespoon pure vanilla extract
3	tablespoons virgin olive oil
2	egg whites
1	cup fresh blueberries
6	strawberries, for garnish

Spray butter, whipped cream, and blueberry syrup, for topping

In a large mixing bowl, combine Bisquick, milk, vanilla, and olive oil; mix. Whip egg whites by hand until they are light and fluffy. Add egg whites and blueberries to Bisquick mix and whip slightly. Refrigerate overnight. If mixture is too thick, just add a little milk, and whip.

Pour about ½ cup of the mixture onto a waffle iron and cook until done, about 5 minutes. Garnish the plates around the waffles with strawberries. Spray liquid butter on top of the waffle. Add whipped cream to the center of the waffle. Drizzle with blueberry syrup.

Jacob's Resting Place

B uilt two centuries ago as a colonial tavern-inn called The Sign of the Green Tree, this pristine brick Georgian offered respite to travelers. Now, Jacob's Resting Place occupies the same quarters on the same three acres at the edge of Carlisle. Trout continue to thrive in the Letort stream that is on the property.

In the formal foursquare garden, the brick walkways are Jeffersonian in design, and are lined with American Boxwood. The octagonal cottage garden is filled with medicinal and culinary herbs, dye plants, and ornamentals. The center area garden is covered with oyster shells that were dug while planting the garden. Oysters brought up the Susquehanna River were a staple on the original tavern menu. After serving, the shells were tossed out the back door where they remained for 200 years.

Terry Heglin, present-day innkeeper at Jacob's Resting Place, is a Civil War historian, and a wonderful resource to tap before a trip to the nearby Military History Institute.

INNKEEPERS:	Terry and Marie Hegglin
ADDRESS:	1007 Harrisburg Pike
	Carlisle, Pennsylvania 17013
TELEPHONE:	(717) 243-1766; (888) 731-1790
E-MAIL:	jacobsrest@pa.net
WEBSITE:	www.jacobsrestingplace.com
ROOMS:	5 Rooms; 4 Suites; Private baths
CHILDREN:	Age 12 and older welcome
PETS:	Not allowed

Stuffed Ham Crêpes

Makes 10-12 Crepes

"When guests arrive at breakfast, they are seated at a table set with china, crystal, and silver. Their first course of fresh fruit will be served immediately."
~ Innkeeper, Jacob's Resting Place 1790 Bed & Breakfast

Batter:

1	cup flour, sifted
2	tablespoons sugar
1½	teaspoons baking powder
2	eggs, beaten slightly
1¼	cups milk

Filling:

12	slices honey ham
1½ - 2	cups Jack cheese, grated

Cream Sauce:

¼	cup sweet butter
¼	cup flour
1½	cups whole milk, warmed

Salt, to taste
Nutmeg, to taste

Combine and beat all of the batter ingredients. Let batter sit for one hour before making the crêpes. Spray a crepe pan or small frying pan with cooking spray before making each crêpe. Put enough batter in the pan so that it thinly covers the bottom of the pan. When the top of the batter loses its shine, turn the crêpe over. It only takes 1-2 minutes. Remove from the pan when the second side loses its shine. Keep warm and covered while cooking the remaining crêpes.

For the filling: Place one slice of ham on a crêpe and put cheese along one edge; roll. Place crêpes on a warm pan, cover, and keep warm in a 150°F oven.

For the cream sauce: Heat butter and flour enough to brown the flour. Add warm milk to the flour mixture, beating until the sauce becomes thick. Sauce consistency should be similar to heavy cream. Add nutmeg and salt, to taste, before serving.

Egg Dishes & Breakfast Entrées

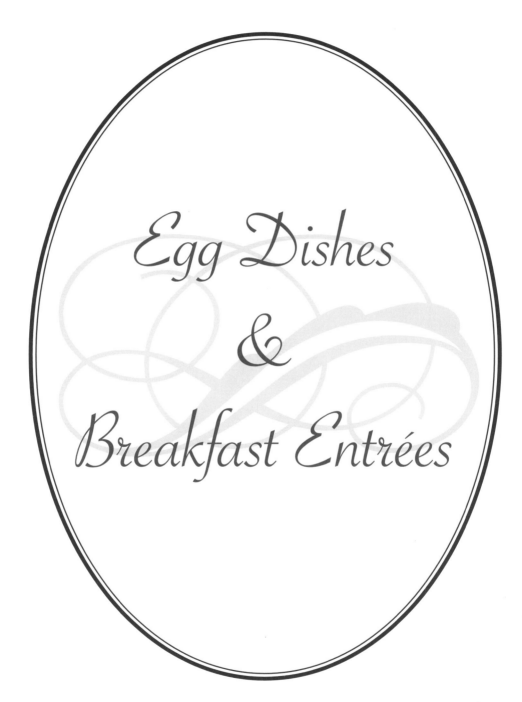

Egg Dishes

&

Breakfast Entrées

Three Gables Inn

Three Gables Inn is a Victorian Sears Catalogue house built in 1895 in Elgin, just seven miles from Corry. It is one of over 100,000 homes ordered from the Sears Roebuck Catalogue in the early 1900s and assembled by the owners. The fact that many of the homes are still in existence today attest to the quality and design of their construction. At Three Gables Inn, the oak and chestnut woodwork complement the high ceilings. The dining room floor is unique with its alternating strips of cherry and maple wood. Treasures from the owner's travels to Thailand, China, Italy, and Australia are displayed throughout the home.

"We visited Lake Chautauqua, Lake Erie, a winery, Blair, the first oil well museum, and other sites in the area with helpful directions supplied by our hostess. The best part of our stay was the delightful Victorian decorated home of Peggy, who most graciously served a sumptuous, hearty breakfast each day." ~ Guest

INNKEEPERS:	Peggy Paul
ADDRESS:	18323 South Main Street
	Corry, Pennsylvania 16407
TELEPHONE:	(888) 640-5487
E-MAIL:	Not available
WEBSITE:	www.threegablesinn.net
ROOMS:	3 Rooms; Private baths
CHILDREN:	Welcome
PETS:	Not allowed

Open Faced Quiche

Makes 6 Servings

"This quiche is great for breakfast or lunch." ~ Innkeeper, Three Gables Inn

1	large English Muffins
1	pound Swiss cheese, grated
¼	cup fresh basil, chopped
3	large eggs
⅔	cup half & half
⅛	teaspoon nutmeg
⅛	teaspoon cayenne pepper
½	teaspoon salt

Split, toast, and butter the muffins. Place on baking sheet butter side up.

Combine grated cheese and basil in a bowl. In a separate bowl, beat eggs, half & half, and seasonings. Pour over cheese mixture. Spread mixture over muffins. Broil briefly until bubbly. Watch carefully to avoid burning.

Belle Reve

"Where a Dream and a River Meet" is the innkeeper's slogan for Belle Reve, an historic riverside bed and breakfast in the Village of Riverton.

The Delaware River is an amenity for travelers staying at the inn. Many of the rooms in this 1843 Greek Revival farmhouse have river views. The riverfront gazebo invites guests to while away the hours. A new Belle Reve dock on the banks of the Delaware provides the perfect stopover opportunity for river kayakers The bed and breakfast is at the foot of a bridge that leads to the tiny town of Belvidere. Walk or bicycle across the span, and you'll find a pretty-as-a-picture-postcard blend of finely maintained Colonial and Victorian mansions. The winter holiday lights are exquisite at the Belle Reve. Of course, the sparkling lights are multiplied by their reflection on the Delaware River.

INNKEEPERS:	Shirley K. Creo
ADDRESS:	7757 Martins Creek-Belvidere Road
	Bangor, Pennsylvania 18013
TELEPHONE:	(610) 498-2026; (888) 549-8608
E-MAIL:	bellereve@enter.net
WEBSITE:	www.bellereveriverside.com
ROOMS:	4 Rooms; 1 Suite; Private baths
CHILDREN:	Age 14 and older welcome
PETS:	Not allowed

Oeufs Extraordinaire

Makes 10 Servings

"Divide the recipe in half to accommodate a smaller crowd. This may be prepared the day before and refrigerated."~ Innkeeper, Belle Reve

Prepare First:

1½	dozen eggs; hard boiled and sliced
1	pound of bacon, fried crisp and crumbled
2	cups of coarse, buttered breadcrumbs

Cheese Sauce:

¼	cup butter
¼	cup flour
2	cups of half & half, hot, but not boiling
¼	teaspoon dried thyme
¼	teaspoon dried basil
¼	teaspoon garlic powder
½	teaspoon salt
½	teaspoon pepper
¼	cup parsley, chopped
1	pound, cheddar cheese, grated

Preheat oven to 350°F. Whisk butter and flour over medium-low heat until flour turns a light brown, about 2 minutes. Add the remaining ingredients, whisking over medium heat until cheese has melted. Grease a 9x13-inch casserole dish. Place a layer of sliced eggs on the bottom of dish, sprinkle with bacon crumbs, and add sauce. Repeat this 2-3 times, ending with the sauce. Cover top with buttered breadcrumbs.

Bake for 20-30 minutes.

Bed and Breakfast on the Park

In Penn's Common Historical District, and across from Penn's Common City Park, is the Queen Anne Victorian mansion that is home to the Bed & Breakfast on the Park. Decorated with antiques and family heirlooms, the warm character of the inn is brought to life by the fun-loving and caring innkeepers, Cindy and George Heminitz.

Built in 1887, the mansion retains its original woodwork, medallions, parlor chandeliers, and second floor-landing chandelier. On Friday evenings during the summer months, settle into a rocking chair on the wrap-around porch, and enjoy concerts in the City Park Band shell.

"Your home was beautiful, immaculate, and the stories were great. This was an experience that left me with permanent memories." ~ Guest

INNKEEPERS:	Cindy and George Heminitz
ADDRESS:	1246 Hill Road
	Reading, Pennsylvania 19602
TELEPHONE:	(610) 374-4440
E-MAIL:	parkbandb@enter.net
WEBSITE:	www.parkbandb.com
ROOMS:	4 Rooms; 1 Cottage; Private and shared baths
CHILDREN:	Age 12 and older welcome
PETS:	Not allowed

Good Morning Pie

Makes 8 Servings

"This needs to be refrigerated overnight after cooking. It also freezes well."
~ Innkeeper, Bed & Breakfast on the Park

2	**cups cottage cheese**
3	**eggs**
$\frac{2}{3}$	**cup sugar**
2	**tablespoons flour**
$\frac{1}{3}$	**teaspoon cinnamon**
$\frac{1}{4}$	**teaspoon nutmeg**
2	**teaspoons orange zest**
1	**tablespoon orange juice**
$\frac{1}{8}$	**teaspoon vanilla**

Fresh fruit, for garnish

Preheat oven to 350°F. Beat the cottage cheese with an electric mixer for 1 minute. Add the remaining ingredients. Blend well. Pour into a greased 9-inch pie plate.

Bake for 50 minutes or until a knife inserted comes out clean.

Refrigerate overnight. Serve chilled with a fresh fruit garnish.

The Bucksville House

Weary travelers are still welcomed at the 1795 Bucksville House in Kintnersville, once a stagecoach stop on the route between Philadelphia and Easton. A registered Bucks County Historical Landmark, the Bucksville House served as a hotel in 1830, and a tavern and speakeasy during the prohibition period. Innkeepers Barbara and Joe Szollosi purchased the Bucksville House as an "ultimate handyman's special" in 1984 and began welcoming guests a year later.

Nearly 100 quilts are displayed throughout the bed and breakfast. The earliest homespun quilt, circa 1800, is one of the treasures in their collection. Guests may meander through the four-acre site, which includes brick and wooden patios, a screened gazebo, and a stocked pond with a walking bridge. Gardeners will love the water garden, perennial flowerbeds, grape arbor, vegetable plot, and the herb garden patterned after a similar one in Colonial Williamsburg. Guests are served breakfast in front of a walk-in fireplace or in the gazebo.

INNKEEPERS:	Joe and Barb Szollosi
ADDRESS:	4501 Durham Road, Route 442
	Kintnersville, Pennsylvania 18930
TELEPHONE:	(610) 847-8948; (888) 617-6300
E-MAIL:	Not available
WEBSITE:	www.bucksvillehouse.com
ROOMS:	4 Rooms; 1 Suite; Private baths
CHILDREN:	Age 12 and older welcome
PETS:	Not allowed; Resident cats

Savory Eggs

Makes 6 Servings

Adapted from *American Country Inn and Bed and Breakfast Cookbook, Vol. 1*

"This recipe may be made the night before and refrigerated until morning."
~ Innkeeper, Bucksville House

2	**cups cheddar cheese, grated**
¼	**cup butter**
1	**cup light cream**
½	**teaspoon salt**
¼	**teaspoon pepper**
2	**teaspoons prepared mustard (spicy brown is preferred)**
12	**eggs, beaten**

Preheat oven to 325°F. Spread cheese in a greased, 9x13-inch pan. Dot with butter. Combine cream and spices. Pour ½ of mixture over the cheese. Pour beaten eggs over ½ of the cream and spices mixture. Add the remaining cream and spices mixture.

Bake for 40 minutes.

The Brickhouse Inn

Gettysburg's historic downtown is well represented by the Brickhouse Inn, an 1898 three-story brick Victorian, along with the adjacent Welty House, built it 1830. The National Battlefield Park is virtually at your doorstep, and Lincoln Square in the town center is only a few minutes away. The area's shops are filled with Civil War collectibles.

The Brickhouse Inn was once the home of a local banker and his family. The historic Welty House, built by Solomon Welty, was in the thick of fighting during the Battle of Gettysburg. Its walls still bear the scars of bullets. Guest accommodations are named for the states represented in the battle at Gettysburg.

The breakfasts are plentiful and delicious. The menu changes daily, but the morning fare always includes the signature dish, Pennsylvania Dutch Shoo Fly Pie. Lemonade and homemade cookies are served in the afternoon.

INNKEEPERS:	Tessa Bardo, Brian Duncan, and Melanie Driscoll
ADDRESS:	452 Baltimore Street
	Gettysburg, Pennsylvania 17325
TELEPHONE:	(717) 338-9337; (800) 864-3464
E-MAIL:	stay@brickhouseinn.com
WEBSITE:	www.brickhouseinn.com
ROOMS:	13 Rooms; 2 Suites; Private baths
CHILDREN:	Age 10 and older welcome
PETS:	Not allowed

Country Breakfast Casserole

Makes 10 Servings

*"You can, but don't have to, refrigerate this overnight. If you do,
be sure to pull the casserole out twenty minutes before you cook it."*
~ Innkeeper, Brickhouse Inn

1	tablespoon butter
4	cups shredded hash browns
12	eggs
1	pint small curd cottage cheese
1/3	cup flour
1	teaspoon baking powder
1/2	teaspoon salt
1	teaspoon white pepper
1/2	cup Parmesan cheese, grated
1	cup cheddar cheese, grated
1/2	pound sausage or bacon, cooked and crumbled

Preheat oven to 350°F. Melt butter in a large skillet. Add potatoes and cook until browned and tender. Add salt and pepper, to taste. Beat eggs in a large bowl. Add cottage cheese, flour, baking powder, salt, and pepper. Whisk.
Stir in cheeses, potatoes, and meat. Pour into a greased 9x13-inch baking pan.

Bake for 30 minutes until set in the center.

The Inn at Narrows Creek

Mother Nature is at her finest in this grove of shagbark hickory trees on the banks of Narrows Creek. The Inn, built in 1998, is the re-creation of an eighteenth-century New England country inn and tavern, in a lovely forest setting. Narrows Creek guests may enjoy leisurely breakfasts in their room and daydreams in the hammock, accompanied by the sounds of trickling waterfalls.

The Narrows Creek Country store offers many wares to make your home cozier and your garden bright. Soft dulcimer music plays in the store as you consider the primitive folk art, country furniture, and one-of-a-kind birdhouses. Many of the items on display are created right on the premises.

"...We truly believe an angel brought us here. What an enchanting evening we spent listening to music, enjoying the sights and sounds of the beautiful garden, and talking in the gazebo by candlelight. This is a slice of heaven and the angels tucked us in. We can't wait to return!" ~Guest

INNKEEPERS:	Henry and Linda Shaffer
ADDRESS:	Route 255 North, 44 Narrows Creek Lane
	DuBois, Pennsylvania 15801
TELEPHONE:	(814) 371-9394
E-MAIL:	theinn@narrowscreek.com
WEBSITE:	www.narrowscreek.com
ROOMS:	2 Rooms; 3 Suites; Private baths
CHILDREN:	Welcome in the Cabin Suite only
PETS:	Call ahead; Resident dog

Company Eggs

Makes 4 Servings

"This recipe must be refrigerated overnight."
~ Innkeeper, Inn at Narrows Creek

4-5	slices of Italian bread
$\frac{1}{2}$ - $\frac{2}{3}$	cup cheddar cheese, grated
4	eggs
2	cups milk
Dash of salt and pepper	
$\frac{1}{2}$	teaspoon dry mustard
4-5	slices of bacon, cooked and crumbled

Lightly grease a 2-quart baking dish with cooking spray. Spread bread pieces over the bottom of the pan. Sprinkle with grated cheese. Mix eggs, milk, salt, pepper, and dry mustard in a medium bowl. Pour egg mixture over bread and cheese. Sprinkle with bacon. Cover and refrigerate overnight.

In the morning, preheat oven to 350°F. Bake uncovered for 40 minutes until golden and crusty.

Limestone Inn

The porch swing is the best spot to watch wildlife at The Limestone Inn. Four miles from Pennsylvania State University, this brick Federal-style 1800 farmhouse is the best spot in town for prospective PSU students, parents visiting students, and alumni to gather for an overnight stay. There is even a guest room at the inn decorated in Penn State colors and decor. Mouth-watering breakfasts are served daily. The new "Back Porch" is glass-enclosed, and overlooks a pond, waterfall, and the mountains. It comfortably seats 25 to 30 people for special events.

Nittany Mountain is the scenic background for the college communities of State College and Penn State's University Park Campus. The word "Nittany" is said to have been derived from a Native American term meaning "single mountain." In the 1700s, the first white settlers adopted this term. By the time Penn State admitted its first students in 1857, the word "Nittany" was widely in use.

INNKEEPERS:	Karen Patzer
ADDRESS:	490 Meckley Road
	State College, Pennsylvania 16801
TELEPHONE:	(814) 234-8944; (888) 922-8944
E-MAIL:	kpatzer@psualum.com
WEBSITE:	www.limestoneinn.com
ROOMS:	5 Rooms; Private baths
CHILDREN:	Call ahead
PETS:	Not allowed; Resident cats

Ham and Egg Nests

Makes 4 Servings

4-8	thin slices of Black Forest Ham (or your favorite ham)
8	eggs
2	ounces Brie cheese
8	tablespoons half & half

Hollandaise sauce (we use Knorr)
Whole grain toast
Tomato and/or asparagus spears, for garnish
Hollandaise sauce, for topping

Preheat oven to 375°F. Spray 8 muffin cups with cooking spray. Line each cup with 1-2 slices of ham, forming a "nest." Cut up Brie cheese into 8 chunks. Remove rind from the cheese. Place a piece of Brie into each ham nest. Crack an egg and place on top of the cheese, being careful not to break the yolk. Top with 1 tablespoon of half & half (this helps keep it moist). Bake nests for 15 minutes, or until the eggs are just set.

Serve over whole grain toast. Garnish with a slice of tomato and/or asparagus spears. Top nests with hollandaise sauce.

The Alden House

Enjoy the ambiance of the charming town of Lititz, Pennsylvania, in the heart of Amish Country. The Alden House is an elegant Lancaster County bed and breakfast located in the center of the Lititz Historical District. Linger by the fishpond or in the garden and scan the natural surroundings for the resident heron. Listen for the faint strains of a melody drifting from the guest sitting room. A piano is provided for the guests who are musically inclined.

Each morning, a full gourmet breakfast is served in the dining room of this 1850 brick Federal-style house. Entrees may include the inn's signature dish, Ployes (French Acadian Crêpes) with Wilbur cinnamon drops, ebleskivers, omelets, or quiche. The attention to detail in the food preparation is apparent. Bob is in charge of preparing the fruit dishes. Written in the guest book was this comment: *"Thank you Shirley and Bob, especially for cutting the grapes for us!"*

Don't forget to sample the Wilbur Buds in the candy dish near the front door.

INNKEEPERS:	Bob and Shirley McCarthy
ADDRESS:	62 East Main Street
	Lititz, Pennsylvania 17543
TELEPHONE:	(717) 627-3363; (800) 584-0753
E-MAIL:	inn@aldenhouse.com
WEBSITE:	www.aldenhouse.com
ROOMS:	2 Rooms; 4 Suites; Private baths
CHILDREN:	Age 10 and older welcome
PETS:	Not allowed

Brie and Cranberry Omelet

Makes 1 Serving

"This omelet is a pleasant change from the usual cheese and vegetable combinations. The Brie and cranberries make it an elegant dish, yet it is quick and easy. If you need more than one omelet, just increase the ingredients."
~ Innkeeper, Alden House Bed & Breakfast

2	**large eggs**
1	**tablespoon milk**
2	**slices of Brie cheese, rind removed**
3	**tablespoons of dried cranberries, divided**

Parsley, for garnish

Grease an 8-inch or 10-inch iron skillet, and heat on stove. Whisk eggs and milk until frothy. Pour egg mixture into hot pan. Place pan under broiler until eggs set, about 4 minutes. Place the Brie slices and 2 tablespoons of cranberries on top. Place back under broiler until the cheese melts.

With spatula, fold omelet over and slide onto a warm plate. Garnish with remaining cranberries and parsley.

Classic Victorian

The Classic Victorian Bed and Breakfast is situated in the historic district of the quaint borough of Nazareth, the oldest Moravian community in North America. A Victorian lamppost in front of the inn displays a welcoming sign to announce your arrival at this hospitable destination. Hanging baskets of bright geraniums will greet you on the sweeping front veranda. Inside, the beautiful stained-glass window, coupled with chestnut pocket-doors, is awe-inspiring.

Breakfast at the inn is an event that you don't want to miss. Culinary delights are presented in the eighteenth-century candlelit dining room, with the table set on fine linens with Wedgwood china. The breakfast options requiring advance notice are a fireside morning meal, or an early riser continental breakfast delivered to your door in a basket. In the warmer months, breakfast is offered on the second floor terrace, the wrap-around veranda, or in the fragrant wisteria-covered arbor.

INNKEEPERS:	Irene and Dan Sokolowski
ADDRESS:	35 North New Street
	Nazareth, Pennsylvania 18064
TELEPHONE:	(610) 759-8276
E-MAIL:	classicvictorianbnb@msn.com
WEBSITE:	www.classicvictorianbnb.com
ROOMS:	4 Rooms; Private baths
CHILDREN:	Age 5 and older welcome
PETS:	Not allowed

Breakfast Bake

Makes 6 Servings

8	frozen hash brown patties
1	teaspoon butter, melted
1	teaspoon oil
6	eggs
1	cup milk

Salt and pepper, to taste

$\frac{1}{2}$	cup mozzarella cheese, grated (or your favorite cheese)
1	package bacon, cooked and crumbled
6	slices of tomato

Cook hash browns according to package directions.

Preheat oven to 350°F. Grease medium pan with butter and oil. Line pan with hash brown patties. Whisk the eggs, milk, salt, and pepper. Add grated cheese. Pour mixture over hash browns. Sprinkle bacon on top of egg dish. Bake for 30 minutes. Add tomato slices. Continue cooking until top of breakfast bake is brown, about 15-20 minutes longer. If necessary, cover loosely with foil to keep from over browning.

Creekside Inn

T wo stone tablets in the wall of the Creekside Inn Bed and Breakfast read, "Bilt by David and Esther Witmer" and "In the year of our Lord 1781." This eighteenth-century Georgian limestone home will welcome you as it did George Washington over 200 years ago. Built on 2 acres, the Creekside Inn property is part of an original William Penn land grant, peacefully situated along the Pequea Creek in the village of Paradise.

The Mennonite Church built its first meetinghouse in 1806 on land contributed by David Witmer, the village innkeeper, who was a member of the Mennonite congregation. The church tolerated the fact that David Witmer was an innkeeper, but several years after the church had been built, he was excommunicated because he used a carriage with "springs."

INNKEEPERS:	Cathy and Dennis Zimmermann
ADDRESS:	44 Leacock Road
	Paradise, Pennsylvania 17562
TELEPHONE:	(717) 687-0333; (866) 604-2574
E-MAIL:	cathy@thecreeksideinn.com
WEBSITE:	www.thecreeksideinn.com
ROOMS:	4 Rooms; 1 Suite; Private baths
CHILDREN:	Unable to accommodate
PETS:	Not allowed

Pineapple Egg Casserole

Makes 6 Servings

Adapted from *Bisquick Cookbook*

"This dish is wonderful served with a thick slice of ham."
~ Innkeeper, Creekside Inn Bed & Breakfast

1	cup Bisquick
4	eggs
1	teaspoon dried mustard
$\frac{1}{8}$	teaspoon nutmeg
1	cup milk
6	tablespoons butter, melted
$\frac{1}{2}$	teaspoon onion powder
1	(8-ounce) can crushed pineapple, drained
1	cup Monterey Jack cheese, grated

Preheat oven to 350°F. Whisk first 7 ingredients in a large bowl until smooth. Stir in pineapple and cheese. Pour into a greased 9-inch pie plate.

Bake for 35-40 minutes.

Failte Inn

Failte (pronounced Fall-Cha) is the Gaelic word for welcome.

Failte Inn is in the Susquehanna River Valley amid the Endless Mountains of rural Pennsylvania. The site of the inn overlooks acres of green lawns, apple orchards, flower gardens, and fountains. Feel the cool mountain breezes during the lazy days of summer, or warm up in front of a fireplace in the parlor or well-stocked library on a cool winter's day. Listen to the quiet, or compose your own fine music on the antique baby grand piano.

The Failte Inn offers complimentary carafes of Mead (honeyed wine) from days of old in their private pub, which was operated as a speakeasy during the days of Prohibition. There is an outdoor spa where you can soak as you stargaze. The on-site antique shop specializes in finer Victoriana.

INNKEEPERS:	Jim, Sarah, and Jamie True
ADDRESS:	RR# 2 Box 323 Sheshequin
	Athens, Pennsylvania 18810
TELEPHONE:	(570) 358-3899
E-MAIL:	thefailteinn@webtv.net
WEBSITE:	www.failteinn.com
ROOMS:	5 Rooms; 2 Suites; Private baths
CHILDREN:	Welcome
PETS:	Not allowed; Resident cat

Vegetarian Strata

Makes 2 Servings

"This recipe needs to be made the night before and kept in the refrigerator."
~ Innkeeper, Failte Inn

4	slices bread (homemade sourdough, if possible)
2	tablespoons apricot jam (or other jam, if preferred)
2	tablespoons cream cheese, softened
3	eggs
¾	cup milk

Salt and pepper, to taste

½	teaspoon vanilla

Coat a small baking dish with cooking spray. Spread cream cheese and jam on 2 slices of bread. Place in bottom of baking dish with cream cheese and jam side up. Cover with the remaining 2 bread slices. Mix eggs, milk, salt, pepper, and vanilla. Pour over bread layers. Refrigerate overnight.

In the morning, preheat oven to 350°F.

Bake for 45 minutes.

Morgan Century Farm

Established in 1850 as a family farm, the original farmhouse, one barn, and two outbuildings still remain on the Morgan Century Farm grounds. A small milk house built in the 1930s now serves as a potting shed. In 1995, great-great granddaughter, Linda Faye Morgan, and her husband Ken Florentine began a three-year restoration of the main building as a country inn. Being antique car lovers, with a special interest in Plymouths, Ken and Linda named each guest room in the main house after a Plymouth model of the early 1950s. A rustic two-story cottage, meant just for two, is another lodging choice at Morgan Century Farm. Or, you may want to consider the old barn hayloft with its deck extending out above Elks Creek. The Elegant Duck Gift Shop is located in the lower part of the barn.

Each morning, a three-course breakfast is served, with complimentary wine and cheese offered in the afternoon.

INNKEEPERS:	Ken and Linda Florentine
ADDRESS:	Route 1 Lincoln Falls
	Forksville, Pennsylvania 18616
TELEPHONE:	(570) 924-4909; (888) 335-1583
E-MAIL:	morcenfm@epix.net
WEBSITE:	www.pa-bedandbreakfast.com
ROOMS:	5 Rooms; 1 Cottage; Private baths
CHILDREN:	Unable to accommodate
PETS:	Welcome in the cottage; Resident cat

Eggs McMorgan

Makes 5 to 6 Servings

"This is a quick and easy vegetable frittata."
~ Innkeeper, Morgan Century Farm Bed & Breakfast

1	cup chopped broccoli
½	cup green onions, sliced
1	(16-ounce) can diced tomatoes, drained
1	tablespoon fresh basil, chopped
6	large eggs, well beaten

Salt and pepper, to taste
½	cup extra sharp cheddar cheese, grated

Coat the skillet with cooking spray and heat to medium-high. Sauté the broccoli and onions until tender. Add tomatoes and basil. Heat through. Pour eggs over broccoli/tomato mixture. Add salt and pepper, to taste.

Cover and cook for 15 minutes over low heat. Sprinkle with cheese and heat until cheese is melted.

Casa DaCosta

There is a dramatic view of the Mercer County Courthouse from the outdoor patio at the Casa DaCosta Bed & Breakfast. A baby grand piano, a marble-inlaid fireplace, and a crystal chandelier create a lovely view for the guests who are lounging on camelback sofas in the living room. The Victoria, Belle Vista, and Shenandoah guestrooms allow one to feel that it's yesterday once more.

Cheese strata and lemon poppy scones are two of the breakfast specialties served to the guests staying in this two-story, brick, Greek-revival home. Inquire about the tea parties for groups of four to fifteen. Sample the delicate finger sandwiches and sweet pastries, accompanied by your choice of tea. Gift baskets are available upon request.

"This house was built in 1929 by Lucille Webster, whom
we like to fancy still roams the halls." ~Innkeeper

INNKEEPERS:	Caroline L. DaCosta
ADDRESS:	116 West Market Street
	Mercer, Pennsylvania 16137
TELEPHONE:	(724) 662-5681; (888) 824-3763
E-MAIL:	casadacosta@zoominternet.net
WEBSITE:	www.casadacosta.net
ROOMS:	2 Rooms; 1 Suite; Private and shared baths
CHILDREN:	Unable to accommodate
PETS:	Not allowed; Resident dog

Ham and Cheese Strata

Makes 6 to 8 Servings

Adapted from *Pampered Chef*

"This recipe is so easy to prepare. It is one of our most requested breakfast items. It must be refrigerated overnight."
~ Innkeeper, Casa DaCosta Bed & Breakfast

8	slices of bread, cubed
4	ounces sharp cheddar cheese, cubed
1	cup ham, cubed
6	eggs
2	cups milk
$\frac{1}{2}$	teaspoon dry mustard
$\frac{1}{2}$	teaspoon salt
1	teaspoon onion flakes
4	ounces cheddar cheese, grated

Preheat oven to 375°F. Lightly grease a 9x13-inch pan. Place $\frac{1}{2}$ of the bread cubes in the pan. Place cubed cheese and ham over bread. Add remaining bread. In a separate bowl, beat eggs, milk, dry mustard, salt, and onion flakes until combined. Pour egg mixture over bread, ham, and cheese. Cover with cheese. Refrigerate overnight.

In the morning, preheat oven to 375°F. Bake for 45 minutes or until set. Cut into wedges and serve.

Vogt Farm

Cows with calves at their sides; roaming Herbie the bull; ducks greeting the dawn; moonlight over the fields ... this is Vogt Farm, a gentleman's farm in the fertile lands of Lancaster County. Mennonites built the house and dairy barn in 1868. The west side of the barn was executed in a fancy brick design, and unlike most bank barns, it opens to the north. Guestrooms are named for people of significance to the farm's past. There is the Barbara and Samuel Suite, and the Gramma and Grampa, Brubaker, Cousin Edith, and the Witmer Rooms.

"Thanks for the enjoyable stay as usual. What a relaxation from the limelight! I guess I will see you again next year. What do you think about a movie about Lancaster County?" ~ Tom Hanks, guest

INNKEEPERS:	Keith and Kathy Vogt
ADDRESS:	1225 Colebrook Road
	Marietta, Pennsylvania 17547
TELEPHONE:	(717) 653-4810; (800) 854-0399
E-MAIL:	stay@vogtfarmbnb.com
WEBSITE:	www.vogtfarmbnb.com
ROOMS:	3 Rooms; 1 Suite; Private baths
CHILDREN:	Age 7 and older welcome
PETS:	Not allowed

Potato, Egg, Cheese, & Ham

Makes 8 Servings

Adapted from *Lancaster County Central Market Cookbook*

"This dish is so easy and tasty that everyone wants the recipe. You fix it the night before, and just bake it in the morning." ~ Innkeeper, Vogt Farm

6	cups hash browns
Minced onion, to taste	
Salt, to taste	
8	eggs, beaten
2	cups ham, cubed
1½	cups mild cheddar cheese, grated

Lightly grease a 9x11-inch baking dish with cooking spray. Put potatoes, onion, and salt in the dish; stir to combine. Pour beaten eggs over the potato mixture. Top with ham and sprinkle with cheese. Cover and refrigerate overnight. In the morning, preheat oven to 350°F. Remove cover from baking dish and bake for 1 hour. Serve hot.

Cresson House

The spacious grounds of the classic Colonial Cresson House are just minutes away from I-99, and 180 miles northwest of Washington D.C. This tastefully decorated inn is nestled in the Allegheny Mountains of Central Pennsylvania.

The Cresson area is a popular destination for railroad buffs: Tunnels Park and Museum is immediately adjacent to the Gallitzen Tunnels; the Heritage Park observation platform, and Pennsylvania Railroad Caboose are in Derry. Nearby Altoona is home to the Horseshoe Curve National Historic Landmark and the Railroader's Memorial Museum. Another local attraction, the Mount Assisi Gardens, is cultivated on the palatial grounds of former steel baron Charles Schwab. The Franciscans who now occupy the mansion maintain this Italian formal garden.

INNKEEPERS:	Marti Stefanon
ADDRESS:	417 Park Avenue
	Cresson, Pennsylvania 16630
TELEPHONE:	(814) 886-5014
E-MAIL:	cressonhouse@verizon.net
WEBSITE:	www.cressonhouse.com
ROOMS:	5 Rooms; Private bath
CHILDREN:	Welcome
PETS:	Not allowed

Vegetarian Quiche

Makes 8 Servings

1	cup sour cream
1	cup milk
18	eggs, beaten
2	teaspoons salt
$\frac{1}{2}$	cup green onions, chopped
$\frac{1}{4}$	cup green peppers, diced
$\frac{1}{4}$	cup red peppers, diced
1	cup cheddar cheese, grated
$\frac{1}{4}$	cup butter, melted

Preheat oven to 350°F. Melt butter. Combine sour cream, milk, and eggs in a large bowl and mix. Add salt, onions, peppers, and cheese; mix well. Stir in melted butter. Pour into a lightly greased, deep, 9x13-inch baking dish.

Bake for 35 minutes.

The Alden House

Enjoy the ambiance of the charming town of Lititz, Pennsylvania, in the heart of Amish Country. The Alden House is an elegant Lancaster County bed and breakfast located in the center of the Lititz Historical District. Linger by the fishpond or in the garden and scan the natural surroundings for the resident heron. Listen for the faint strains of a melody drifting from the guest sitting room. A piano is provided for the guests who are musically inclined.

Each morning, a full gourmet breakfast is served in the dining room of this 1850 brick Federal-style house. Entrees may include the inn's signature dish, Ployes (French Acadian Crêpes) with Wilbur cinnamon drops, ebleskivers, omelets, or quiche. The attention to detail in the food preparation is apparent. Bob is in charge of preparing the fruit dishes. Written in the guest book was this comment: *"Thank you Shirley and Bob, especially for cutting the grapes for us!"*

Don't forget to sample the Wilbur Buds in the candy dish near the front door.

INNKEEPERS:	Bob and Shirley McCarthy
ADDRESS:	62 East Main Street
	Lititz, Pennsylvania 17543
TELEPHONE:	(717) 627-3363; (800) 584-0753
E-MAIL:	inn@aldenhouse.com
WEBSITE:	www.aldenhouse.com
ROOMS:	2 Rooms; 4 Suites; Private baths
CHILDREN:	Age 10 and older welcome
PETS:	Not allowed

Herb Shirred Eggs

Makes 1 serving

"One morning, I found out at the last minute that our guests could not eat what I had planned. I remembered preparing shirred eggs in my "college waitress" days. To spice them up, I took a quick look at my spices and herbs and came up with this winner. Guests love them!" ~ Innkeeper, Alden House Bed & Breakfast

1	teaspoon butter
1	large or jumbo egg
1	"sprinkling" (1/8-1/4 teaspoon) Montreal Chicken Seasoning (McCormick Grill Mates)
1	"sprinkling" (1/8-1/4 teaspoon) parsley flakes

Preheat oven to 400°F. Put butter in a custard cup. Place in the oven until butter melts. Break egg into the cup, being very careful not to break the egg yolk. Sprinkle with chicken seasoning and parsley flakes. You may vary the amount of seasonings, to taste. Bake for approximately 10 minutes. Egg is done when yolk is still slightly soft to the touch.

Serve immediately.

The Bucksville House

Weary travelers are still welcomed at the 1795 Bucksville House in Kintnersville, once a stagecoach stop on the route between Philadelphia and Easton. A registered Bucks County Historical Landmark, the Bucksville House served as a hotel in 1830, and a tavern and speakeasy during the prohibition period. Innkeepers Barbara and Joe Szollosi purchased the Bucksville House as an "ultimate handyman's special" in 1984 and began welcoming guests a year later.

Nearly 100 quilts are displayed throughout the bed and breakfast. The earliest homespun quilt, circa 1800, is one of the treasures in their collection. Guests may meander through the four-acre site, which includes brick and wooden patios, a screened gazebo, and a stocked pond with a walking bridge. Gardeners will love the water garden, perennial flowerbeds, grape arbor, vegetable plot, and the herb garden patterned after a similar one in Colonial Williamsburg. Guests are served breakfast in front of a walk-in fireplace or in the gazebo.

INNKEEPERS:	Joe and Barb Szollosi
ADDRESS:	4501 Durham Road, Route 442
	Kintnersville, Pennsylvania 18930
TELEPHONE:	(610) 847-8948; (888) 617-6300
E-MAIL:	Not available
WEBSITE:	www.bucksvillehouse.com
ROOMS:	4 Rooms; 1 Suite; Private baths
CHILDREN:	Age 12 and older welcome
PETS:	Not allowed; Resident cats

Onion Quiche

Makes 6 Servings

Adapted from Culinary Institute of America Cookbook

2	tablespoons olive oil
$2\frac{1}{2}$	cups yellow onions, sliced
$\frac{3}{4}$	cup heavy cream
$\frac{3}{4}$	cup milk
3	large eggs
$\frac{1}{2}$	teaspoon salt
$\frac{1}{4}$	teaspoon pepper
$1\frac{1}{4}$	cups provolone cheese, grated
1 9-inch unbaked piecrust	

Preheat oven to 350°F. Sauté onions in oil until a golden color, about 15 minutes. Remove onions from pan. Whisk cream, milk, eggs, salt, and pepper in a large bowl. Stir onions and 1 cup of cheese into the egg mixture. Pour this mixture into the piecrust. Sprinkle the remaining cheese on top of the quiche.

Bake for 40-45 minutes or until knife inserted in center comes out clean.

Elver Valley Farm

Rolling dairy farmland and woodland provide the natural environment for the Elver Valley Farm ranch-style Guest Home and Acorn Rock Cabin. Streams and greenery are plentiful in this area between Brandywine Valley and the Lancaster County Dutch Country. From the breakfast table, a dozen different varieties of birds may be observed. Chester County mushrooms can be requested as a part of a full breakfast.

Walk down the winding driveway to Acorn Rock Cabin, and you'll pass the children's swing and slide playground. The cabin overlooks a half-acre pond alive with frogs and fish. You are welcome to take a swim or row out in the boat and go fishing. Picnic tables are conveniently located for a meal outside. A pasture with assorted farm animals to feed and pet are in full view of the cabin.

INNKEEPERS:	Elvin and Vera Rohrer
ADDRESS:	432 Sawmill Road
	Cochranville, Pennsylvania 19330
TELEPHONE:	(717) 529-2803; (877) 863-5837
E-MAIL:	evrohrer@webtv.net
WEBSITE:	www.pafarmstay.com/elvervalley
ROOMS:	2 Rooms; 1 Cottage; Private baths
CHILDREN:	Welcome
PETS:	Not allowed

Cheese Bacon Squares

Makes 8 to 10 Servings

"I serve this at my Bed and Breakfast as the main part of the meal."
~ Innkeeper, Elver Valley Farm

1	**(8-ounce) package refrigerated crescent rolls**
¼	**cup mozzarella cheese, grated, or Monterey Jack cheese, grated**
¾	**cup Swiss cheese, grated**
1	**egg, beaten**
¾	**cup milk**
¼	**cup onion, finely chopped**
½	**cup mushrooms, chopped**
6	**slices bacon, cooked and crumbled**
1	**tablespoon minced parsley**

Preheat oven to 350°F. Separate crescent dough into two rectangles and place in a 9x13-inch pan. Press the dough into the bottom and sides of the pan to form a crust. Sprinkle cheeses over dough.

Combine egg, milk, onion, and mushrooms. Pour over cheeses. Sprinkle with bacon and parsley.

Bake 25 minutes or until crust is golden brown and egg is cooked.

Hamanassett

The historic registry mansion of Hamanassett in the Brandywine Valley continues a centuries-old tradition of hospitality, one guest at a time. Past and present converge the moment you enter the Grand Hall.

"...located on the top and slope of a fine hill with more than three-fourths of the land covered with a luxuriant growth of noble woods...it was modeled on Downings Northern Farmhouse built of hard, dark gray stone taken from the land...and he chose the Indian name of a small river by which his forefathers had settled [in 1647], and he called it 'HAMANASSETT'."
From the Memoir of Dr. Charles D. Meigs (1792-1869)
The description is still accurate today.

"...A perfect retreat away from the world and into a secret garden." ~ Guest

"The elaborate breakfasts are a high point." ~ New York Times

INNKEEPERS:	Ashley Mon
ADDRESS:	115 Indian Springs Drive
	Chester Heights, Pennsylvania 19017
TELEPHONE:	(610) 459-3000; (877) 836-8212
E-MAIL:	stay@hamanassett.com
WEBSITE:	www.hamanassett.com
ROOMS:	5 Rooms; 2 Suites; and Carriage House; all private baths
CHILDREN:	Age 12 and older welcome; Under age 12 allowed in Carriage House
PETS:	Welcome in the Carriage House; Resident pet

Baked Cheese Grits

Makes 8 Servings

"Our guests love this dish, as long as we do not tell them it is grits!"
~ Innkeeper, Hamanassett Bed & Breakfast

4	cups whole milk
$\frac{1}{2}$	stick unsalted butter
$\frac{1}{4}$	teaspoon salt
$\frac{1}{4}$	teaspoon black pepper
1	cup quick grits (not instant!)
4	large eggs, beaten
4	cups cheddar cheese, grated

Preheat oven to 350°F. Place milk, butter, salt, pepper, and grits in a 2-3 quart saucepan. Cook until grits are thick and creamy. Add eggs to grits, a little at a time, stirring after each addition. Stir in cheese by handfuls until completely melted. Pour into a well buttered 8 or 9-inch cake pan. Bake for 40 minutes until top is brown. Let cool.

If this dish is not served immediately, cover with foil and refrigerate. It can be sliced into serving pieces and frozen. To serve, bring to room temperature, and microwave on high for about 40-60 seconds.

Sayre Mansion Inn

S ayre Mansion is the Lehigh Valley's premier urban inn. Located in the heart of Bethlehem's Fountain Hill Historic District, the mansion was originally the home of town icon and entrepreneur, Robert Sayre. One of eighteen guest rooms, the fabulous Conservatory Room, offers a 180-degree bird's-eye-view of Bethlehem. Spanning the full depth of the house, this rooftop refuge may be the most unique room in the house. But also comparable is the Library Room, featuring a large bedroom and separate sitting room/library with the original vaulted ceiling and chandelier. This literary haven contains two floor-to-ceiling bookcases and a gas fireplace surrounded in marble.

To start your day off right, help yourself to the breakfast buffet of fresh fruit, home-baked muffins, breads, and pastries. The Sayre Mansion offers a selection of hot breakfast entrees. Fresh-squeezed orange juice and rich-roasted coffee complement the delightful morning fare.

INNKEEPERS:	Carrie Ohlandt
ADDRESS:	250 Wyandotte Street
	Bethlehem, Pennsylvania 18015
TELEPHONE:	(610) 882-2100; (877) 345-9019
E-MAIL:	innkeeper@sayremansion.com
WEBSITE:	www.sayremansion.com
ROOMS:	18 Rooms
CHILDREN:	Welcome
PETS:	Welcome in one room

Baked Eggs in a Puff Pastry

Makes 6 Servings

12	puff pastry shells, frozen		1	egg
6	tablespoons half & half		½	teaspoon thyme
1	teaspoon minced onion		1	teaspoon dill
1	teaspoon chives, chopped			
1	teaspoon parsley plus an additional 1 tablespoon, for garnish			

Salt and pepper, to taste
8   tablespoons butter
4   tablespoons flour
½   cup roasted garlic flavored chicken broth (plain chicken broth will work)
½   cup heavy cream
½   cup Comte Cheese, grated (may substitute Asiago)
1   (16-ounce) bag diced potatoes with onions
1   (16-ounce) bag southwest style hash browns
Bacon, for topping; Strawberries, for garnish

Preheat oven to 375°F. Place the frozen puff pastry shells on baking sheet. Bake for 25-30 minutes or until golden brown. Set aside to cool.

While puff pastry is cooking, melt 4 tablespoons of butter in a large sauté pan. Add both bags of potatoes; stir to coat well with butter. Cover and cook over medium heat for 20 minutes or until uniformly browned, stirring occasionally. Set aside in a warm place. Melt remaining 4 tablespoons of butter in a medium saucepan. Add flour and whisk for approximately 1 minute. Add chicken broth and heavy cream to butter and flour mixture, whisking constantly until thickened and starting to bubble.

Add grated cheese and stir until completely melted. Remove from heat, cover and set aside in a warm place.

Combine thyme, dill, chives, parsley, and minced onion in a small bowl; set aside. Remove pastry tops from puff pastry. Fill each shell with one egg. Add ½ tablespoon of half & half to each pastry shell, being careful not to overfill the shells. Sprinkle salt and pepper over egg/cream mixture in shells. Replace pastry tops; sprinkle herb mix over each puff pastry shell. Bake for 20 minutes until eggs are soft, but fully cooked. Remove from oven.

Place 2 of the puff pastries on a plate and drizzle with cheese sauce. Sprinkle with parsley for garnish. Serve with approximately ¾ cup of potato mixture and several slices of bacon. Garnish with strawberries.

Blue Ball

In spring and fall, watch the Amish farmers plant and harvest their crops from the Blue Ball Bed & Breakfast, located in the scenic Lancaster County countryside. Visit Amish woodworking, quilt, furniture, and craft shops. Dining with an Amish family may be arranged in advance. After a full day, unwind in the 6-person Jacuzzi in an enclosed patio attached to the inn. Thoughtful details abound at the Blue Ball Bed & Breakfast: soft terry robes and slippers, and delightfully thick towels.

The inn is minutes away from Sight and Sound American Music Theatre, museums, antique stores, and factory outlet shopping. Blue Ball B & B is just a short distance from the towns of Intercourse, Bird-in-Hand, and Paradise. Quilting weekends are available.

INNKEEPERS:	Frank and Jeanne Warsheski
ADDRESS:	1075 Main Street
	Blue Ball, Pennsylvania 17506
TELEPHONE:	(717) 355-9994; (800) 720-9827
E-MAIL:	pudone@ptd.net
WEBSITE:	www.blueballbandb.com
ROOMS:	4 Rooms; 2 Suites; Private baths
CHILDREN:	Welcome
PETS:	Small pets allowed; Resident cat

Country Sausage Gravy & Rolls

Makes 10 Servings

"...A good breakfast item that can be made the night before and reheated using a little more milk." ~ Innkeeper, Blue Ball Bed & Breakfast

1	**pound breakfast sausage**
1	**pound turkey sausage**
1	**pound sweet Italian sausage**
4	**cups milk**
3	**tablespoons flour**
Salt and pepper, to taste	
2	**(10-count) refrigerated dinner rolls**

Brown all of the sausages, cutting into small pieces while frying. Add the milk and warm on low heat. Mix flour with a small amount of cold water to make a paste. Gradually add paste to the sausage mixture and thicken to desired consistency. Add salt and pepper, to taste.

Prepare rolls per package directions. Serve sausage gravy over the rolls.

Keystone Inn

Keystone Inn is in a residential area of Gettysburg, away from the commercialism and busyness of downtown, but only five blocks from Lincoln Square. Built by a local furniture maker in 1913, the quality craftsmanship is evident in this late Victorian-style brick home. A wide-columned porch hugs the north and west sides of the house. Inside the huge leaded-glass main entrance, you'll see the chestnut staircase marching majestically to the third floor. Copious amounts of natural oak and chestnut are found throughout the house. Chestnut was used almost exclusively in the first floor rooms, and oak is found in abundance in the rest of the house. The quiet guestrooms stand behind massive, two-inch thick doors.

"We slept like lambs." ~ Guest

"This place is cleaner than my mother-in-laws place,
and she's the 'Queen of Clean.' "~ Guest

INNKEEPERS:	Doris and Wilmer Martin
ADDRESS:	231 Hanover Street
	Gettysburg, Pennsylvania 17325
TELEPHONE:	(717) 337-3888
E-MAIL:	keystoneinnbb@yahoo.com
WEBSITE:	www.keystoneinnbb.com
ROOMS:	4 Rooms; 1 Suite; Private baths
CHILDREN:	Welcome
PETS:	Not allowed

Hash Brown Casserole

Makes 6 to 8 Servings

"...A wonderful breakfast or brunch entrée. Serve with fruit, and you have all of the food groups. It is absolutely delicious!"~ Innkeeper, Keystone Inn

6	eggs
2	cups milk
1/4	teaspoon pepper
1	tablespoon spicy mustard
1/2	onion, chopped
1/4	bell pepper, chopped
1	cup broccoli, chopped
1	cup sharp cheddar cheese, grated
1	(16-ounce) bag hash browns
1	cup cooked ham, chopped

Preheat oven to 350°F. Combine eggs, milk, pepper, and mustard in a large bowl. Mix well. Add remaining ingredients and mix thoroughly. Pour into a greased 9x13-inch baking dish. Bake uncovered for 45 minutes or until knife inserted in middle comes out clean.

Soups, Salads, & Side Dishes

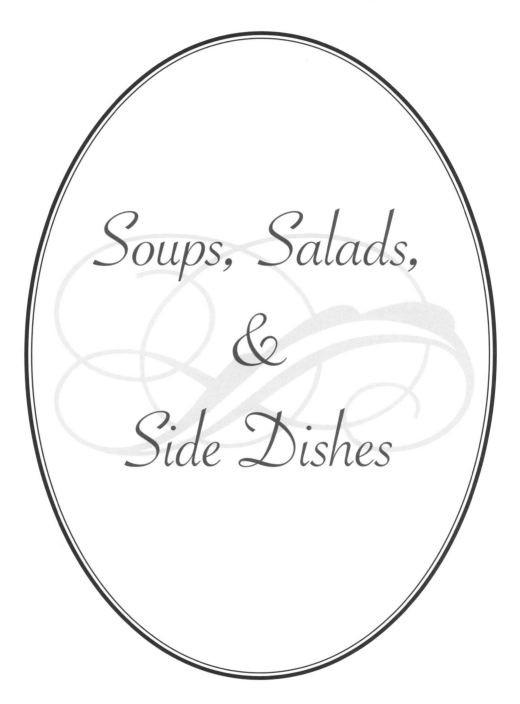

Soups, Salads, & Side Dishes

Flowers & Thyme

All variations of the colors lavender and pink enhance the acre of countryside that is home to Flowers & Thyme. From early spring until late fall, perennial flowers mixed with annuals, plus the herb gardens create a colorful and lush vision for guests of the inn. "We've been featured in the *Birds & Blooms* magazine, but it's the thoughtful comments from our guests that we cherish the most," say the innkeepers.

Built in 1941, the brick Colonial house was constructed by an Amish man for a Mennonite family. Cheery, eclectic furnishings lend an air of elegant simplicity to Flowers & Thyme. The large, commodious Gathering Room has a vaulted ceiling and an expanse of windows overlooking a peaceful valley with a working farm. Bountiful breakfasts are served in this room. Aromas from snow pea garden breakfast quiche, French toast with southern fried apples, or eggs scrambled with a rich chicken sauce may be wafting through the inn as you awaken.

INNKEEPERS:	Don and Ruth Harnish
ADDRESS:	238 Strasburg Pike
	Lancaster, Pennsylvania 17602
TELEPHONE:	(717) 393-1460
E-MAIL:	Innkeeper@flowersandthyme.com
WEBSITE:	www.flowersandthyme.com
ROOMS:	3 Rooms; Private baths
CHILDREN:	Age 12 and older welcome
PETS:	Not allowed

Jalapeño Sweet Potato Soup

Makes 14 Cups

"We tasted this in a little cafe in Texas and loved it. We asked for, and were given, the recipe to take back to Pennsylvania to try on our own. The original recipe called for 2 tablespoons of pickled jalapeño juice, which I omitted - a bit too spicy for us.
~ Innkeeper, Flowers & Thyme Bed & Breakfast

2	tablespoons butter
3	slices bacon, finely chopped
1	medium onion, chopped
3	cloves garlic, minced
4	pounds sweet potatoes, peeled and cubed
8	cups chicken broth
¼	cup pickled jalapeños plus 2 tablespoons pickled jalapeño juice, for a spicier soup
1	teaspoon cumin
¼	teaspoon baking soda
½	cup chopped cilantro
1½	cups half & half
1	teaspoon salt
1	teaspoon pepper

Melt butter in a soup pot over medium heat. Add bacon, onion and garlic; cook until bacon is crisp and onions are soft. Add sweet potatoes, chicken broth, pickled jalapeños, and cumin. Bring to a boil, cover, lower heat, and simmer until potatoes are tender. Add baking soda, cilantro, and half & half to pot. Coarsely mash potatoes with a potato masher or a handheld immersion blender. Stir well, and season with salt and pepper.

1833 Umpleby House

Prominent mill owner, William Umpleby, built the Classical Revival plaster-over-stone Umpleby Manor House in 1833. When his grain mill was completely destroyed by fire, Umpleby decided to rebuild, giving the town "new hope." This picturesque riverside village was named New Hope to celebrate Umpleby's optimistic reconstruction.

Conveniently located in the historic district, Umpleby House features 26-inch thick walls, wide pumpkin pine floors, and deep-set windows overlooking fields, a creek, and a wooded hillside. Guest rooms are individually painted and stenciled by a New Hope artist and are graced with fresh cut flowers all year 'round. Umpleby House offers the perfect setting for either business or pleasure, and can accommodate groups of three to thirty for meetings and retreats.

INNKEEPERS:	Carl and Nadine Glassman
ADDRESS:	117 West Bridge Street
	New Hope Historic District, Pennsylvania 18938
TELEPHONE:	(215) 862-3936
E-MAIL:	info@1833umplebyhouse.com
WEBSITE:	www.1833umplebyhouse.com
ROOMS:	6 Rooms; 1 Suite; 1 Cottage; Private baths
CHILDREN:	Age 12 and older welcome
PETS:	Not allowed

Cucumber Soup

Makes 8 Servings

5	cucumbers
1	onion
1	(10½-ounce) can chicken broth
2	sprigs fresh dill plus 8 sprigs, for garnish
1½	teaspoon fresh basil
1⅓	cups sour cream

Salt, to taste

Peel the cucumbers and cut lengthwise; remove seeds. Place the seeded cucumbers in a blender. Add the onion, broth, dill, and basil; blend well. Add the sour cream and mix. Add the salt.

Refrigerate for several hours. Garnish with fresh dill sprigs and serve cold.

Aaron Burr House

The Aaron Burr House takes its name from the third vice president of the United States. After Aaron Burr's infamous and fatal pistol duel with Alexander Hamilton in 1804, Burr escaped to New Hope seeking a safe haven. The inn's foundation is all that remains of the original pre-Revolutionary War era home where Burr is said to have hidden for a week. Today, the Aaron Burr house provides a warm and friendly atmosphere for weary city dwellers seeking escape to rural Bucks County.

"Wow! I had a fight with my honey the same week, but 200 years apart from Burr's duel with Hamilton. The Burr and Hamilton families took 200 years to end their feud. With the help of this big, lace canopy bed, we kissed and made up in two minutes. New Hope is for lovers, and the Aaron Burr House is the best place to kiss." ~ Guest

The tree-shaded corner location and the large, screened-in flagstone patio reflect the peaceful atmosphere at the Aaron Burr House. "Fresh is best" is the innkeepers' motto regarding breakfast.

INNKEEPERS:	Jess and Nadine Sill
ADDRESS:	80 West Bridge Street
	New Hope Boro, Pennsylvania 18938
TELEPHONE:	(215) 862-2520
E-MAIL:	stay@aaronburrhouse.com
WEBSITE:	www.aaronburrhouse.com
ROOMS:	6 Rooms; 1 Suite; 1 Cottage; Private baths
CHILDREN:	Age 12 and older welcome
PETS:	Not allowed

Western New Hope Chili

Makes 8 Servings

*"Sometimes I substitute turkey for buffalo. Both have very little fat.
Out here on the west bank of the Delaware River, the Wedgwood
Collection of Inns is located on the western edge of New Hope, where
it is said the women are strong and the men are good lookin'.
They like their chili hot, spicy, and heart healthy too. I like to serve this
chili on cold wintry afternoons with a thick slice of black bread."*
~ Innkeeper, Aaron Burr House

1	pound ground buffalo (substitute lean ground beef, if buffalo is not available or desired)
2	medium onions, chopped
2	cloves garlic, minced
1	green pepper, chopped
1	yellow pepper, chopped
1	(28-ounce) can tomatoes
1	(16-ounce) can dark kidney beans
1½	tablespoons Worcestershire sauce
1	tablespoon vinegar
1⅓	teaspoons dry mustard
1	teaspoon sugar
1	teaspoon kosher salt
1	teaspoon red pepper
½	teaspoon black pepper
⅔	teaspoon chili pepper

In a stockpot, brown the ground meat with the onions, garlic, and peppers.
Drain. Add the remaining ingredients. Simmer for several hours.

Gettystown Inn

Historic Dobbin House Tavern is located next door to Gettystown Inn.

Historic Civil War era homes: Leister House, Victorian House, Remembrance House, and Little Round Top Farm provide your accommodations at the Gettystown Inn. The inn is ideally situated, overlooking the spot where Lincoln gave his Gettysburg Address. Lodging includes a superior breakfast served in the sunny parlor of the Dobbin House located next door.

The Dobbin House is Gettysburg's oldest and most historic building. Reverend Alexander Dobbin, a minister and rugged individual who played a major role in the founding of Gettysburg, built it in 1776. The house was already 87-years-old when Lincoln delivered his famous speech. In the mid-1800s, a secret crawl space beneath the authentic, colonial tavern served as a station for hiding runaway slaves on the Underground Railroad. Today, patrons of the Dobbin House may eat, drink, and be merry in the lively spirit of America's beginnings.

INNKEEPERS:	Rick Beamer
ADDRESS:	89 Steinwehr Avenue
	Gettysburg, Pennsylvania 17325
TELEPHONE:	(717) 334-2100
E-MAIL:	info@dobbinhouse.com
WEBSITE:	www.dobbinhouse.com
ROOMS:	5 Rooms; Private baths
CHILDREN:	Age 5 and older welcome
PETS:	Not allowed

Dobbin House Baked King's Onion Soup

Makes 6 Servings

6	cups beef stock
2	tablespoons sweet butter
6	medium onions, peeled and diced
1	cup stewing beef, cut into $\frac{1}{2}$-inch cubes
1	cup dry sherry
6	slices good-quality white bread
12	slices Swiss cheese
12	slices provolone cheese

Bring beef stock to a slow boil in a large saucepan. In a skillet, melt butter and sauté onions until the onions begin to yellow. Brown the beef in a separate skillet. Add onions, beef, and sherry to the stock and simmer for 30 minutes.

When ready to serve, fill 6 ovenproof bowls with soup. Place 1 slice of bread, 2 slices of Swiss cheese, and 2 slices of provolone, in that order, on top of each serving. Place under broiler until cheese browns.

The Beechmont

S ince the time Andrew Jackson was president of the United States, The Beechmont has been on the tree-lined street of stately homes in Hanover. A beautiful 140-year old Magnolia tree is the centerpiece of the garden.

Watch the flames dance in the marble fireplace of the Magnolia Suite, or swing open the door of the Garden Gate Suite and step into a whimsical courtyard. Your imagination will be filled with scenes of regal families and days of simpler living. "Ambiance personified" is how one guest described The Beechmont.

Strains of soft classical music in the background will accompany your breakfast in the dining room. Gather at the large table for some great conversation with fellow travelers, or choose a candlelit table for two. Wherever you are seated, Beechmont baked apples, spice pancakes with lemon sauce, Beechmont buttermilk pie, or an herb cheese tart will be sure to please your palate.

INNKEEPERS:	Kathryn and Thomas White
ADDRESS:	315 Broadway
	Hanover, Pennsylvania 17331
TELEPHONE:	(717) 632-3013; (800) 553-7009
E-MAIL:	innkeeper@thebeechmont.com
WEBSITE:	www.thebeechmont.com
ROOMS:	4 Rooms; 3 Suites; Private baths
CHILDREN:	Age 6 and older welcome
PETS:	Not allowed

Hamburger Soup

Makes 6 to 8 Servings

2	pounds lean ground beef
4	tablespoons olive oil or unsalted butter
1	large onion, peeled and chopped, about 1 cup
1½	cups celery, chopped
2	cloves garlic, minced
1½	teaspoons dried basil
1	teaspoon black pepper
3	medium potatoes, peeled and cubed
2	(14-ounce) cans diced tomatoes, undrained
2½	cups tomato juice
¼	cup Worcestershire sauce
½	teaspoon Tabasco sauce
1	cup water

Brown ground beef in 2 tablespoons of olive oil. Drain. In large pot, add remaining olive oil, onion, celery, garlic, basil, and black pepper. Sauté over medium heat until onions are transparent, about 5 minutes. Add beef, potatoes, tomatoes, tomato juice, Worcestershire sauce, Tabasco sauce, and a cup of water. Simmer over medium heat until potatoes are tender, about 30 minutes.

Mountain Dale Farm

"Mountain Dale Farm is a salvage artist's collection of recycled buildings transformed into comfortable, charming lodging. The collection of unique buildings is set on a farm stage complete with lush fields and grazing cattle. Jack's Mountain forms a perfect backdrop as the lighting of the heavens sets the mood both day and night." ~Innkeeper

A restored 200-year-old log home, cabins, and several rooms in the large farmhouse comprise the lodging facilities at the 175-acre Mountain Dale Farm. The Great Room's décor is eclectic with muzzleloaders, icons, and other interesting artifacts creating the effect of a private museum. The walls are covered with paintings, many done by local artists. Sheep, cattle, horses, ducks, geese, goats, pigs, turkeys, peacocks, chickens, and many cats keep the residents busy on the farm. Thousands of acres of state forestland border the property.

INNKEEPERS:	Ken and Sally Hassinger
ADDRESS:	330 Hassinger Way
	McClure, Pennsylvania 17841
TELEPHONE:	(570) 658-3536
E-MAIL:	mountaindale@mountaindale.net
WEBSITE:	www.mountaindale.net
ROOMS:	4 Rooms; 8 Cottages; Private and shared baths
CHILDREN:	Welcome
PETS:	Not allowed; Many resident pets on the farm

Cashew Nut Loaf

Makes 6 Servings

"...A great dish for your vegetarian guests. However, you can substitute beef broth for meat lovers and they will find it a delicious alternative to traditional meatloaf. A powdered form of broth, or even a powdered beef soup mix, would work. The innkeeper recommends a brand that may or may not be available in your area. It is G. Washington Rich Brown Seasoning & Broth. It has a vegetarian base."
~ Innkeeper, Mountain Dale Farm

1	**cup raw cashews**
2	**stalks celery**
1	**large onion**
1	**teaspoon parsley, minced**
1	**package of powdered vegetarian broth**
2	**cups dried breadcrumbs**
$\frac{1}{2}$	**teaspoon salt**
$\frac{1}{4}$	**cup milk**

Preheat oven to 375°F. Chop or mash the cashews into small pieces. Dice the celery and onion. Combine these ingredients in a bowl. Add the remaining ingredients and mix thoroughly. Add approximately $\frac{1}{4}$ cup of milk to help form the loaf. Place in a loaf pan and bake for 45 minutes.

Golden Pheasant Inn

"A bite of France in Bucks County" ~ *Innkeeper*

Romantic lodging is available at the 1857 fieldstone Golden Pheasant Inn. All rooms have 1850s period style decor and afford a view of the Delaware River and canal. The Golden Pheasant Inn, listed on the National Register of Historic Places, was built as a mule barge stop to service travelers on the canal.

Michel Faure, one of the region's finest chefs, presents his creative country French cuisine in three traditionally restored dining rooms. The romantic setting of the Tavern Room features a fireplace, beamed ceiling, an exposed stonewall, and a brightly colored collection of Quimper Pottery from Brittany, France. The Blaise Room offers quiet, intimate dining. The canal, which is iluminated at night, can be seen from the candlelit, converted greenhouse dining area.

"'Exquisite' is the word to describe this experience." ~*Philadelphia Inquirer*

INNKEEPERS:	Barbara and Michel Faure
ADDRESS:	763 River Road
	Erwinna, Pennsylvania 18920
TELEPHONE:	(610) 294-9595; (800) 830-4474
E-MAIL:	Barbara@goldenpheasant.com
WEBSITE:	www.goldenpheasant.com
ROOMS:	5 Rooms; 1 Cottage; Private baths
CHILDREN:	Age 8 and older welcome
PETS:	Welcome in the Cottage

Risotto with Tomato

Makes 8 Servings

2	cups chicken stock
4	tablespoons unsalted butter
3	tablespoons olive oil
1½	cups white onion, diced
3	garlic cloves, finely chopped
1½	cups short-grained white rice
1	(20-ounce) can Roma tomatoes, pureed with their juices
3	ounces oil-packed, sun dried tomatoes, drained and chopped
2	tablespoons fresh mint leaves, chopped
3	tablespoons Parmesan cheese, grated
Salt	
Pepper, freshly ground	
2	ounces Parmesan cheese, grated, for topping

Pour stock into a saucepan and bring to a simmer. In a heavy saucepan over medium heat, melt 3 tablespoons of butter and mix with the oil. Add the onions and sauté until onions begin to caramelize, about 12 minutes. Add garlic and sauté for 2 minutes. Add rice and stir until each grain is coated with the oil and butter, about 2-3 minutes. Add the pureed and sun-dried tomatoes. Cook and stir until the puree is absorbed.

Ladle in just enough of the stock to nearly cover the rice; stir over medium heat until the stock is absorbed. Add more stock to nearly cover, and continue to stir until the stock is absorbed. Repeat this process, but never completely cover the rice with stock, and never add more stock until the previous stock is absorbed. Cook until the rice is al dente. This process will take about 25 minutes from start to finish. If rice is cooked, and you still have stock left over, that is fine. You may not need all of it.

Add the remaining 1 tablespoon butter, mint, and grated cheese. Add salt and pepper, to taste. Stir to blend. Remove from heat, cover, and let stand 2 minutes. Sprinkle grated Parmesan over the top and serve.

Green Beans Niçoise

Makes 8 Servings

1	pound green beans, washed and patted dry
½	cup olive oil
2	shallots, minced
1	clove garlic, minced
2	cups red tomatoes, chopped
½	cup celery, chopped
1	teaspoon salt
	Black pepper, freshly ground
1	cup chicken stock
1	teaspoon oregano, minced
1	teaspoon basil, minced
¼	cup flat leaf parsley, chopped

Place 4 quarts of water in a 6 quart pot. Add salt, cover, and bring to a boil. Add beans and return to boil. Cook 5-8 minutes. Drain and set aside.

Heat the oil in a large saucepan. Add shallots and garlic and sauté until soft. Add tomatoes, celery, salt, pepper, and chicken stock. Simmer uncovered for 20 minutes. Add oregano, basil, parsley, and green beans. Add salt and pepper, to taste. Stir and serve hot.

Provençal Mesclun with Goat Cheese Salad

Makes 8 Servings

2	tablespoons balsamic vinegar
2	tablespoons lemon juice
2	garlic cloves, crushed
6	tablespoons hazelnut or walnut oil

Salt

12	ounces mesclun or variety of salad greens

Optional salad items: red onion, cucumber, ripe tomato, red bell pepper

6	ounces French goat cheese with crumbly texture
2	cups garlic croutons

Mix vinegar, lemon juice, and garlic. Whisk in the oil. Add salt, to taste. Set aside.

Place salad greens and any additional salad ingredients on plates. Crumble goat cheese and croutons on top of the greens. Pour dressing over individual salads.

Dressing may be made in advance and kept refrigerated in jar. Always shake before using on salad.

The Inn on Maple Street

"The Family and Pet Friendly Bed & Breakfast"

One block from historic Route 6, in the mountains of northwest Pennsylvania's McKean County, you'll find the Inn on Maple Street. Cookies come fresh from the oven at this bed and breakfast, and fireflies dance on the lawn at night. Make your entrance through the unusual banker's door that has a stained-glass side panel in the prairie design of Frank Lloyd Wright. You'll see the stately old upright piano to appease guest's lyrical moods, and an impressive oak staircase. A classic chess set is ready for a match of wits in the Library Room. Shelves of paperbacks are for the taking, with a "take one, leave one" philosophy. The focus of the Parlor Room is on electronic entertainment and big bowls of popcorn. In each guestroom, you'll find tall windows with shutters and lace curtains, and a hand-crocheted afghan on every bed.

"...Outstanding Breakfast," is one guest's reaction to the breakfast buffet by candlelight in the Breakfast Room.

INNKEEPERS:	Jay D. Roush
ADDRESS:	115 Maple Street (one block off Route 6)
	Port Allegany, Pennsylvania 16743
TELEPHONE:	(814) 642-5171
E-MAIL:	innonmaplest@pennswoods.net
WEBSITE:	www.theinnonmaplestreet.com
ROOMS:	4 Rooms; 1 Suite; Private & shared baths
CHILDREN:	Welcome
PETS:	Welcome; Resident dog

Creamed Potatoes on the Half Shell

Makes 6 Servings

"Prepare these a day or two before a big dinner for a time saver. Bake in the oven with the entrée." ~ Innkeeper, Inn on Maple Street

6	large russet potatoes, scrubbed
½	cup sour cream
1	stick butter, softened
½	cup milk
3	tablespoons chopped chives or green onions
2	teaspoons ground pepper
2	teaspoons salt
½	cup cheddar cheese, finely grated

Paprika, for garnish

Preheat oven to 400°F. Bake the potatoes whole for 45-60 minutes. Cool completely. Reduce oven temperature to 350°F. Cut the cooled potatoes in half lengthwise and scoop out flesh, creating a boat or shell with the skin intact. Put potato flesh in a mixing bowl and beat until only slightly lumpy. Add sour cream, butter, milk, chives, pepper, and salt; beat well. Add the cheese and beat just until combined. Fill potato shells with creamed potato mixture. Dust tops with paprika. Put potatoes on a baking sheet and bake for 45-60 minutes.

Mountain Dale Farm

"Mountain Dale Farm is a salvage artist's collection of recycled buildings transformed into comfortable, charming lodging. The collection of unique buildings is set on a farm stage complete with lush fields and grazing cattle. Jack's Mountain forms a perfect backdrop as the lighting of the heavens sets the mood both day and night." ~Innkeeper

A restored 200-year-old log home, cabins, and several rooms in the large farmhouse comprise the lodging facilities at the 175-acre Mountain Dale Farm. The Great Room's décor is eclectic with muzzleloaders, icons, and other interesting artifacts creating the effect of a private museum. The walls are covered with paintings, many done by local artists. Sheep, cattle, horses, ducks, geese, goats, pigs, turkeys, peacocks, chickens, and many cats keep the residents busy on the farm. Thousands of acres of state forestland border the property.

INNKEEPERS:	Ken and Sally Hassinger
ADDRESS:	330 Hassinger Way
	McClure, Pennsylvania 17841
TELEPHONE:	(570) 658-3536
E-MAIL:	mountaindale@mountaindale.net
WEBSITE:	www.mountaindale.net
ROOMS:	4 Rooms; 8 Cottages; Private and shared baths
CHILDREN:	Welcome
PETS:	Not allowed; Many resident pets on the farm

Audrey Barron's Rosemary Potatoes

Makes 6 Servings

"Farm guests rave about these tasty spuds." ~ Innkeeper, Mountain Dale Farm

1/3	cup margarine, melted
1/3	cup salad oil
3	tablespoons lemon juice
2	garlic cloves, peeled
6	large baking potatoes, washed and cut into 1-inch slices
1-2	tablespoons rosemary

Preheat oven to 400°F. Mix margarine, salad oil, lemon juice, and garlic in a blender. Pour mixture into a large bowl with potatoes. Gently toss potatoes to coat. Sprinkle with rosemary. These potatoes may be grilled for 10 minutes on each side, or spread on trays and roast for 30 minutes until lightly browned.

Failte Inn

Failte (pronounced Fall-Cha) is the Gaelic word for welcome.

Failte Inn is in the Susquehanna River Valley amid the Endless Mountains of rural Pennsylvania. The site of the inn overlooks acres of green lawns, apple orchards, flower gardens, and fountains. Feel the cool mountain breezes during the lazy days of summer, or warm up in front of a fireplace in the parlor or well-stocked library on a cool winter's day. Listen to the quiet, or compose your own fine music on the antique baby grand piano.

The Failte Inn offers complimentary carafes of Mead (honeyed wine) from days of old in their private pub, which was operated as a speakeasy during the days of Prohibition. There is an outdoor spa where you can soak as you stargaze. The on-site antique shop specializes in finer Victoriana.

INNKEEPERS:	Jim, Sarah, and Jamie True
ADDRESS:	RR# 2 Box 323 Sheshequin
	Athens, Pennsylvania 18810
TELEPHONE:	(570) 358-3899
E-MAIL:	thefailteinn@webtv.net
WEBSITE:	www.failteinn.com
ROOMS:	5 Rooms; 2 Suites; Private baths
CHILDREN:	Welcome
PETS:	Not allowed; Resident cat

Mexican Eggplant

Makes 6 to 8 Servings

"This spicy vegetable casserole is a real crowd pleaser."
~ Innkeeper, Failte Inn Bed and Breakfast

2	tablespoons cornmeal
2	medium eggplants, peeled and cut into 1-inch cubes
2	cups bread crumbs
2	eggs
1	teaspoon Tabasco sauce

Dash ground red pepper

1	cup sour cream
1	tablespoon jalapeños, chopped
1	small onion, chopped

Salt and pepper, to taste

1	(6-ounce) can green chilies
1-1½	cups cheddar cheese, grated

Preheat oven to 350°F. Grease a 9x9-inch baking dish. Sprinkle the bottom with cornmeal. Boil eggplant until almost cooked. In a large bowl, combine eggplant and the remaining ingredients, except the cheese. Blend well. Scoop into the baking dish and bake for 45-50 minutes. Top with cheese and return to oven until cheese is melted.

Carter Camp Lodge

"One of Nature's Last Outposts"

Located in downtown Carter Camp, population 2, the lodge has provided food and accommodations for wayward travelers for over 150 years. Built in the 1850s as a stagecoach stop, the exterior of the lodge is much as it was at the turn of the century. There are seven guest rooms on the second floor. A sitting room and a large dining area are available for guests to gather and socialize, or relax by the woodstove and unwind. Carter Camp Lodge Café serves a full country breakfast. The store, also on the premises, offers locally produced items, sporting goods, and groceries.

Do you like to hike? Are you tired of carrying your backpack? Use a goat! Goats are coming soon to Carter Camp to help carry your gear.

INNKEEPERS:	John and Barbara Andrews
ADDRESS:	2136 Germania Road
	Galeton, Pennsylvania 16922
TELEPHONE:	(814) 435-1192
E-MAIL:	Not Available
WEBSITE:	www.cartercamplodge.com
ROOMS:	7 Rooms; Private and Shared baths
CHILDREN:	Welcome
PETS:	Not allowed; Resident dog and cat

Broccoli Salad

Makes 6 Servings

"This is a dinner favorite for all of our guests."~ Innkeeper, Carter Camp Lodge

1	**bunch broccoli, cut into bite-size pieces**
1	**onion, diced**
1	**cup mayonnaise**
¼	**cup sugar**
1	**tablespoon vinegar**
8	**ounces mozzarella cheese, grated**
4-6	**slices crisp bacon, crumbled**

Combine broccoli and onion. Mix mayonnaise, sugar, and vinegar. Pour the dressing over broccoli and onion. Toss. Add the cheese and bacon. Toss. Refrigerate about 2 hours before serving. The longer it sits the better it tastes.

The Inn at Starlight Lake

"Sit back, watch the world go by, and remember;
everything is better by Starlight."

The history of The Inn at Starlight Lake began in 1806 when a Connecticut settler named Underwood acquired 10,000 acres of rolling hills in northeastern Pennsylvania. In 1880, his grandson built a dam at the outlet of a small pond, and expanding it into a large body of water he named "Starlight Lake." Eugene Fay bought a tract of land near the eastern shore of the lake in 1907 and built a summer boarding house he called "Starlight Inn."

Today, The Inn at Starlight Lake is very family-friendly, and accommodates visitors in the Main House and three cottages. A plethora of activities, inside, around the inn, and on the lake are available to fulfill the recreation and entertainment needs of guests young, old, and in-between. Breakfast, lunch, and dinner may be enjoyed in the informal lakeside dining room. All pastas and desserts, including ice creams, are made on the premises.

INNKEEPERS:	Sari and Jimmy Schwartz
ADDRESS:	289 Starlight Lake Road
	Starlight, Pennsylvania 18461
TELEPHONE:	(570) 798-2519; (800) 248-2519
E-MAIL:	info@innatstarlightlake.com
WEBSITE:	www.innatstarlightlake.com
ROOMS:	22 Rooms; 1 Suite; Private & shared baths
CHILDREN:	Welcome
PETS:	Welcome

Spinach Tofu Salad Dressing

Makes 3 Cups

½	pound firm tofu, crumbled
1	cup spinach leaves
¼	green bell pepper
1	tablespoon fresh basil, chopped
¼	teaspoon black pepper
1	scallion, chopped
3	tablespoons cider vinegar
¾	teaspoon salt
1	cup vegetable oil

Put all ingredients, except the oil, in a blender or food processor and blend until liquefied. While blender is still running, slowly drizzle a steady stream of oil into the mixture. Chill before serving over your favorite greens.

Hickory Bridge Farm

At the base of the foothills of the Appalachian Mountains, sits the Hickory Bridge Farm. A well-stocked trout stream winds through the farm, which is nine miles west of Gettysburg. Farm-related antiques decorate the late-1700s farmhouse, where deer can be spotted from the large deck in the backyard. Quiet country cottages are positioned in the woods by the creek. A full breakfast is featured Monday through Saturday at the farmhouse, and Continental breakfast baskets are prepared for guests on Sunday.

Since 1977, delicious, bountiful dinners have been served in the restored 180-year-old barn. Linen tablecloths are often adorned with fresh flowers from the garden. The main course of the dinner is presented family-style at your own table, and consists of three entrees, several vegetables, corn fritters, and stewed apples. There is always dessert, and the dessert is always homemade.

INNKEEPERS:	Mary Lynn and Robert Martin
ADDRESS:	96 Hickory Bridge Road
	Orrtanna, Pennsylvania 17353
TELEPHONE:	(717) 642-5261; (800) 642-1766
E-MAIL:	hickory@pa.net
WEBSITE:	www.hickorybridgefarm.com
ROOMS:	7 Rooms; 6 Private baths
CHILDREN:	Welcome; Call ahead
PETS:	Not allowed

Vegetable Pasta Salad

Makes 6 Servings

1	cup uncooked pasta (any appropriate pasta shape will do)
2	small carrots, cut into 2-inch strips
2	green onions, chopped
1	(2-ounce) jar pimiento, drained and diced
¾	cup celery, chopped
¼	cup frozen green peas, thawed
2	tablespoons fresh parsley, chopped
10	cherry tomatoes, halved
¼	cup Italian salad dressing
2	tablespoons mayonnaise
⅛	teaspoon pepper

Cook pasta according to package directions, omitting salt. Drain pasta and rinse with cold water. Combine pasta with remaining ingredients; toss well. Chill at least 1 hour.

Old Fashioned Potato Salad

Makes 6 Servings

Adapted from *a recipe by Joan Ritter*

2	tablespoons flour
2	tablespoons sugar
1	teaspoon salt
1	teaspoon dry mustard
Dash of pepper	
¾	cup milk
2	egg yolks, lightly beaten
¼	cup vinegar
1½	teaspoons butter
8	cups potatoes, cooked and cubed
½	cup onion, chopped
½	cup celery, chopped
4	hard boiled eggs, chopped

Combine flour, sugar, salt, dry mustard, and pepper in a small saucepan. Stir in milk and egg yolks. Cook until bubbly. Set aside. Add vinegar and butter. Cool. Combine potatoes, onion, celery, and eggs in large bowl. Add dressing and mix lightly. Serve chilled.

Cucumbers with Onions

Makes 4 Servings

2	**cups cucumbers, thinly sliced**
½	**cup onions, red or white, thinly sliced**
1	**cup tomatoes, thinly sliced**
¾	**cup white vinegar**
¾	**cup sugar**
1	**teaspoon salt**

Freshly ground pepper, to taste

Arrange the sliced cucumbers, onions, and tomatoes in a flat serving dish. Combine remaining ingredients in a shaker. Shake until sugar is dissolved. Pour over the vegetables and soak at least one hour. To serve, arrange on a salad plate or in small individual bowls. Drizzle any remaining liquid over vegetables.

Field & Pine

Stately pine trees stand guard around this Early American farmhouse. Old boxwoods line the front walkway and gardens. The Field and Pine dwelling dates back to 1790. It was originally built as a tavern called "Sign of the Indian King." The inn has seven fireplaces and wide-plank pine floors. Join your host and other guests for a complimentary beverage, and listen to the innkeepers' stories about local history, traditions, and customs.

This 80-acre working farm includes a barn constructed from local limestone, where the sheep are housed and the grain and hay are stored. Watching the sheep graze on the pasture hill, and leisurely walks through the fields are favorite pastimes at the Field & Pine Bed and Breakfast. Big Spring, a short one-mile hike from the inn, forms one of the most famous limestone fly-fishing streams in Pennsylvania.

INNKEEPERS:	Allan and Mary Ellen Williams
ADDRESS:	2155 Ritner Highway
	Shippensburg, Pennsylvania 17257
TELEPHONE:	(717) 776-7179
E-MAIL:	fieldpine@kuhncom.net
WEBSITE:	www.bedandbreakfast.com/pennsylvania
ROOMS:	3 Rooms; 1 Suite; 2 Shared baths
CHILDREN:	Age 12 and older welcome
PETS:	Not allowed; Resident cat

Spring Asparagus Puffs

Makes 6 Servings

4	tablespoons butter or margarine, divided
2	tablespoons onion, chopped
1	pound asparagus, cut into 1-inch pieces
$\frac{1}{2}$	teaspoon sugar
$\frac{1}{2}$	teaspoon salt
2	tablespoons water
6	eggs
$\frac{1}{3}$	cup heavy cream
$\frac{1}{8}$	teaspoon pepper
$1\frac{1}{2}$	cups cheddar cheese, grated, for topping

Preheat oven to 425°F. Sauté the onion in 2 tablespoons butter or margarine. Add asparagus and sprinkle with sugar and salt. Add 2 tablespoons water, cover and steam for 1-2 minutes. Remove the cover and cook until most of the liquid has evaporated. Set aside to cool slightly. Whisk eggs, heavy cream, and pepper in a bowl until blended. Melt remaining 2 tablespoons of butter or margarine and place in a square 8-inch baking dish. Pour egg mixture into dish and bake for 10 minutes or until bottom sets.

Arrange asparagus mixture on top of eggs and bake for an additional 5 minutes. Remove from oven and top with cheese. Bake 10 minutes longer. Cut into squares and serve.

The Artist's Inn and Gallery

"One of the 25 most romantic inns in the country for Valentine's Day"
~BedandBreakfast.com

The Artist's Inn & Gallery, built in 1848, is a Federal-style home nestled in the small town of Terre Hill and surrounded by Amish and Mennonite farms. The clip-clop of horse drawn buggies as neighbors pass, and the bell chimes from a nearby church are common sounds at the Artist's Inn. Flowerbeds encircle the inn with a broad palette of colors.

Innkeeper Bruce Garrabrandt is a full-time artist. His finely detailed, colored-pencil drawings are on display at the inn. Innkeeper Jan Garrabrand has a passion for cooking and is a self-confessed recipe addict. Everything from the scones in the morning to the chocolates at turndown is made from scratch.

"Jan's breakfasts are fabulous." ~ Guest

INNKEEPERS:	Jan and Bruce Garrabrandt
ADDRESS:	117 East Main St.
	Terre Hill, Pennsylvania (Lancaster County) 17581
TELEPHONE:	(717) 445-0219; (888) 999-4479
E-MAIL:	stacy@artistinn.com
WEBSITE:	www.artistinn.com
ROOMS:	1 Room; 2 Suites; 1 Cottage; Private baths
CHILDREN:	Welcome in the cottage
PETS:	Not allowed; Resident cats

Zucchini Parmesan Squares

Makes 9 Servings

"This appetizer can be made the night before and just reheated in a water bath when ready to bake; also freezes well." ~ Innkeeper, Artist's Inn & Gallery

3	pounds zucchini, trimmed, cut into 1-inch pieces
$\frac{1}{4}$	cup butter, or $\frac{1}{2}$ stick
1	large onion
4	garlic cloves, chopped
2	eggs, beaten
$\frac{1}{2}$	cup Parmesan cheese, grated
$\frac{1}{2}$	cup fresh, white breadcrumbs (if mixture is too soggy, add more)
$\frac{1}{4}$	cup fresh basil, chopped and packed

Additional grated Parmesan cheese, if desired, for topping
Salt and pepper, for seasoning

Preheat oven to 375°F. Butter an 8-inch square baking pan; set aside. Steam the zucchini until tender, about 10 minutes. Transfer zucchini to a large bowl and mash with a fork until a coarse texture. Spoon zucchini into sieve and drain well, pressing to release excess water. Return drained zucchini to bowl.

Melt butter in a heavy, large skillet over medium-high heat. Add onion and garlic; sauté until light brown, about 10 minutes. Add onion mixture to zucchini in bowl. Add eggs, Parmesan, breadcrumbs and basil. Stir to blend well. Add salt and pepper, to taste. Transfer mixture to prepared baking dish. Bake until firm in center and brown on top, about 45 minutes. Cut into squares and serve with additional Parmesan cheese, if desired.

New Hope's 1870 Wedgwood Inn

This Wedgwood-blue Victorian "Painted Lady" is listed on Bucks County Registry of Historic Places. Wedgwood Inn is spelled Wedgwood, not "Wedgewood," because Wedgwood Inn is named after the Englishman, Josiah Wedgwood, who invented the famous Wedgwood-blue bone china. The original portion of the inn served as a campsite for General George Washington and 1,200 Continental Army soldiers in December of 1776, prior to the famous Christmas Eve crossing of the Delaware River.

The inn is located on two private acres in a park-like setting, with flower-lined brick walkways leading to two gazebos and a hammock. New Hope's Historic Village is just steps away. Breakfast is served daily—in bed, on the expansive dining porch, or on one of the Victorian-style covered porches. Homemade goodies are available all day long.

INNKEEPERS:	Carl & Nadine Glassman
ADDRESS:	111 West Bridge Street
	New Hope Historic District, Pennsylvania 18938
TELEPHONE:	(215) 862-2570
E-MAIL:	stay@wedgwoodinn.com
WEBSITE:	www.wedgwoodinn.com
ROOMS:	7 Rooms; 1 Suite; 1 Cottage
CHILDREN:	Age 12 and older welcome
PETS:	Not allowed

Salmon Mousse

Makes 3½ Cups

"We liked to order this dish at the Logan Inn when Carl Lutz and Art Saunders were the chefs/owners. At one point, Carl and I rented an apartment in New Hope from Art in the late seventies, and we would pay our rent and have dinner at the Logan. Because we usually dined there midweek when it was slower, we had a chance to get to know Carl and Art and the locals who hung out in the Tavern Room, which dates back to 1722 or so. We remained friends with them and years later, when we became innkeepers, we enjoyed their overflow referrals. They continued to be our innkeeper mentors until their retirement in 1969."~Innkeepers, Wedgwood Inn

1	(8-ounce) can feta salmon (substitute any canned salmon if feta cannot be found)
1¼	tablespoons lemon juice
3	tablespoons onions, minced
2	(8-ounce) packages cream cheese
¼	teaspoon salt
1¼	tablespoons red horseradish (substitute white, if red cannot be found)

Melba toast rounds, if desired, for serving
Caviar, if desired, for topping

In a serving bowl, combine all ingredients. Chill in the refrigerator for several hours. It can be used as a mousse or as a spread on Melba toast rounds, and may be topped with caviar.

Luncheon & Dinner Entrées

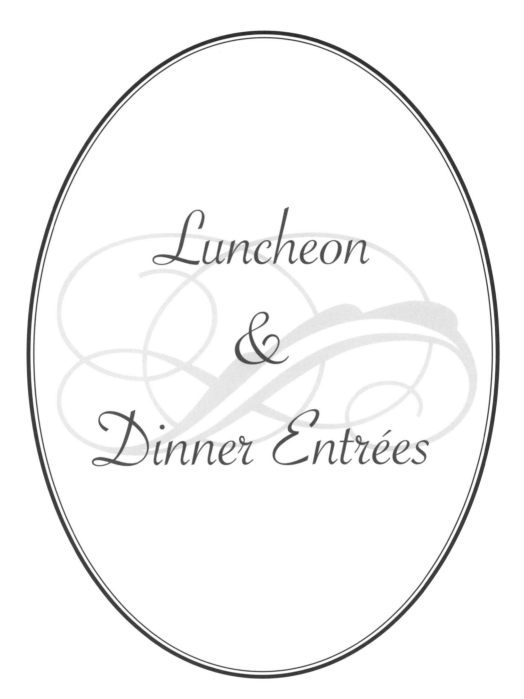

Luncheon

&

Dinner Entrées

1833 Umpleby House

Prominent mill owner, William Umpleby, built the Classical Revival plaster-over-stone Umpleby Manor House in 1833. When his grain mill was completely destroyed by fire, Umpleby decided to rebuild, giving the town "new hope." This picturesque riverside village was named New Hope to celebrate Umpleby's optimistic reconstruction.

Conveniently located in the historic district, Umpleby House features 26-inch thick walls, wide pumpkin pine floors, and deep-set windows overlooking fields, a creek, and a wooded hillside. Guest rooms are individually painted and stenciled by a New Hope artist and are graced with fresh cut flowers all year 'round. Umpleby House offers the perfect setting for either business or pleasure, and can accommodate groups of three to thirty for meetings and retreats.

INNKEEPERS:	Carl and Nadine Glassman
ADDRESS:	117 West Bridge Street
	New Hope Historic District, Pennsylvania 18938
TELEPHONE:	(215) 862-3936
E-MAIL:	info@1833umplebyhouse.com
WEBSITE:	www.1833umplebyhouse.com
ROOMS:	6 Rooms; 1 Suite; 1 Cottage; Private baths
CHILDREN:	Age 12 and older welcome
PETS:	Not allowed

Umpleby's Bumblebee Tuna Egg Pie

Makes 8 Servings

4	eggs
½	teaspoon dry mustard

Few grains cayenne pepper

1½	cups half & half
1	9-inch pastry shell, unbaked
1	(6½-ounce) can tuna, drained and flaked
2	cups grated Swiss cheese
1	teaspoon flour

Preheat oven to 400°F. In a medium bowl, beat eggs, dry mustard, and cayenne pepper until foamy. Beat in the half & half. Cover the bottom of the pastry shell with a layer of tuna. Sprinkle ½ of the cheese over the tuna. Repeat layering. Sprinkle flour over the cheese/tuna mixture. Pour the egg mixture over all. Bake for 35 minutes.

The Beechmont

A BED & BREAKFAST INN

Since the time Andrew Jackson was president of the United States, The Beechmont has been on the tree-lined street of stately homes in Hanover. A beautiful 140-year old Magnolia tree is the centerpiece of the garden.

Watch the flames dance in the marble fireplace of the Magnolia Suite, or swing open the door of the Garden Gate Suite and step into a whimsical courtyard. Your imagination will be filled with scenes of regal families and days of simpler living. "Ambiance personified" is how one guest described The Beechmont.

Strains of soft classical music in the background will accompany your breakfast in the dining room. Gather at the large table for some great conversation with fellow travelers, or choose a candlelit table for two. Wherever you are seated, Beechmont baked apples, spice pancakes with lemon sauce, Beechmont buttermilk pie, or an herb cheese tart will be sure to please your palate.

INNKEEPERS:	Kathryn and Thomas White
ADDRESS:	315 Broadway
	Hanover, Pennsylvania 17331
TELEPHONE:	(717) 632-3013; (800) 553-7009
E-MAIL:	innkeeper@thebeechmont.com
WEBSITE:	www.thebeechmont.com
ROOMS:	4 Rooms; 3 Suites; Private baths
CHILDREN:	Age 6 and older welcome
PETS:	Not allowed

Marinated Chicken Wings

Makes 12 Servings

While this is more appropriately an appetizer, a plate of chicken wings and a beer are considered by "wing aficionados" as "dinner"; often served with celery sticks and ranch dressing on the side.

4-5	pounds of chicken wings (remove wing tips and slice between remaining joint)
1	cup soy sauce
1	cup dry sherry or dry vermouth
2	cloves garlic, minced
¼	cup green onions, chopped, include white and green portions
⅓	cup honey
½	cup pineapple juice
1	teaspoon ground ginger
¼	cup olive oil

Preheat oven to 350°F. Prepare chicken wings. Place wings in a greased, 9x13-inch baking dish. Combine the remaining ingredients in a bowl, and blend thoroughly. Pour marinade over chicken wings and refrigerate for at least 2 hours. Bake for 45 minutes, turning occasionally, until browned and cooked through.

Apple Chicken

Makes 6 Servings

1	whole chicken, cut-up (or about 4 boneless chicken breasts or 4-6 thighs)
8	slices bacon
$\frac{1}{2}$	cup celery, chopped
$\frac{1}{2}$	cup onion, chopped
2	large Granny Smith apples; peeled, cored, and chopped
2-3	tablespoons olive oil
1	cup apple cider
$1\frac{1}{2}$	cups chicken stock
$\frac{1}{2}$	cup white wine
Salt and pepper, to taste	
$\frac{1}{2}$	pint heavy cream
2	tablespoons flour
3	cups rice, cooked

Fry bacon in large skillet until crisp. Remove from skillet and chop. Dust chicken with flour. Leave 1 tablespoon of bacon drippings in the skillet. Place floured chicken in the skillet and brown for 5-6 minutes. Remove chicken from skillet, and set chicken aside.

In the same skillet, add olive oil, celery, and onions. Saute until onions are transparent. Add apples and sauté another 2 minutes. Transfer chicken, bacon, celery, onion, and apple mixture to a large pot or Dutch oven. Add apple cider, chicken stock, and wine. Simmer 40 minutes over low heat. Remove chicken.

In a separate bowl, whisk flour into heavy cream, and add to the large pot. Stir over low heat until the flour and cream mixture have thickened the sauce in the pot. Be sure to keep the temperature low so that the cream does not curdle. Return chicken to the pot after the sauce has thickened and heat through. Serve over rice.

Yummy Chicken

Makes 4 Servings

4	chicken breasts; boneless, skinless
4	ounces cream cheese
2	tablespoons Dijon mustard
2	tablespoons brown sugar
1	tablespoon fresh lemon juice
$\frac{1}{3}$	cup red currant jelly
$\frac{1}{2}$	teaspoon cinnamon
$\frac{1}{3}$	cup sliced almonds
2	cups brown rice, cooked, for serving

Preheat oven to 325°F. Place chicken breasts between two pieces of waxed paper. Using a tenderizing mallet, flatten to about 1/3-inch thickness. Divide the cream cheese into four equal portions and spread each chicken breast with cream cheese. Roll-up each chicken breast and secure with two toothpicks. Place chicken in a baking dish.

Mix the mustard, brown sugar, and lemon juice in a small bowl. Combine this mixture with the jelly in a small saucepan and cook until the mixture becomes a liquid. Add the cinnamon and almonds and cook for 1 additional minute. Remove from heat and pour the mixture over chicken. Bake for 50-60 minutes. Serve over brown rice.

Cameron Estate Inn & Restaurant

The genteel spirit of nineteenth-century America has been recaptured at the Cameron Estate Inn. Fifteen acres of lawns, rose gardens, babbling streams, and woodlands are yours to explore. Stroll through the circa 1805 Mansion built by President McKinley's great grandfather. Many of the 18 spacious guestrooms have wood-burning fireplaces and grand views of the grounds and gardens of the Cameron Estate. This tranquil, off-the-beaten-path getaway is listed on the National Register of Historic Places and is a Lancaster Historic Preservation Trust site.

A fixed-menu breakfast served nice and hot is complementary with each night's stay. Upscale dining is available in a casually elegant atmosphere for dinner only, Wednesday through Sunday, and is the innovative creation of Chef Kelly Shay. Be sure to make dinner reservations when you reserve your room. The restaurant is very popular with the local residents, as well as the Cameron Estate guests.

INNKEEPERS:	Randy Wagner
ADDRESS:	1855 Mansion Lane
	Mount Joy, Pennsylvania 17552
TELEPHONE:	(717) 492-0111; (888) 422-6376
E-MAIL:	info@cameronstateinn.com
WEBSITE:	www.cameronestateinn.com
ROOMS:	16 Rooms; 1 Suite; 1 Cottage; Private baths
CHILDREN:	Age 12 and older welcome
PETS:	Not allowed

Grilled Chicken and Spinach Salad

Makes enough vinaigrette for 10 Salads

For the Vinaigrette Base:

1	3 pound bag of frozen blueberries
1½	cups sugar
¾	cup brown sugar
Zest from 1 lemon, finely minced	
Juice from same lemon	
1	tablespoon cinnamon
¼	teaspoon nutmeg
¼	cup water
1	tablespoon balsamic vinegar

Boil all ingredients in a large saucepan for 40 minutes. Let cool.
Transfer 1½ cups of cooled vinaigrette into blender.

Additional Vinaigrette Ingredients:

¼	cup balsamic vinegar
¼	cup white wine vinegar
1½	cups salad oil (vegetable not olive)

Add vinegars to the vinaigrette base in the blender. Start blender and slowly add 1½ cups oil in a thin stream. Blend well. Pour into a bowl and chill.

Add ¾ cup more of vinaigrette base and mix.

For the Salad: (Individual serving)

1	grilled chicken breast, sliced
3	ounces fresh baby spinach
1½	tablespoons pecans, chopped
1	ounce Parmesan Cheese, grated
2	ounces of the prepared vinaigrette, about ¼ cup
¼	cup fresh blueberries

Mix spinach and ½ of the pecans in an 8-ounce bowl; add dressing and toss. Place dressed spinach on a chilled plate; arrange chicken around the spinach. Garnish with remaining pecans, Parmesan, and fresh blueberries.

Limestone Inn

The porch swing is the best spot to watch wildlife at The Limestone Inn. Four miles from Pennsylvania State University, this brick Federal-style 1800 farmhouse is the best spot in town for prospective PSU students, parents visiting students, and alumni to gather for an overnight stay. There is even a guest room at the inn decorated in Penn State colors and decor. Mouth-watering breakfasts are served daily. The new "Back Porch" is glass-enclosed, and overlooks a pond, waterfall, and the mountains. It comfortably seats 25 to 30 people for special events.

Nittany Mountain is the scenic background for the college communities of State College and Penn State's University Park Campus. The word "Nittany" is said to have been derived from a Native American term meaning "single mountain." In the 1700s, the first white settlers adopted this term. By the time Penn State admitted its first students in 1857, the word "Nittany" was widely in use.

INNKEEPERS:	Karen Patzer
ADDRESS:	490 Meckley Road
	State College, Pennsylvania 16801
TELEPHONE:	(814) 234-8944; (888) 922-8944
E-MAIL:	kpatzer@psualum.com
WEBSITE:	www.limestoneinn.com
ROOMS:	5 Rooms; Private baths
CHILDREN:	Call ahead
PETS:	Not allowed; Resident cats

Chicken and Yorkshire Pudding

Makes 6 to 8 Servings

For the chicken:

$\frac{1}{4}$	cup vegetable oil
$\frac{1}{3}$	cup flour
2	teaspoons salt
$\frac{1}{4}$	teaspoon pepper
$1\frac{1}{2}$	teaspoons leaf sage, crumbled
1	broiler-fryer chicken, about $3\frac{1}{2}$ pounds, cut up

Yorkshire Pudding:

1	cup sifted flour
1	teaspoon baking powder
1	teaspoon salt
$1\frac{1}{2}$	cups milk
3	eggs
$\frac{1}{4}$	cup fresh chopped parsley or 4 teaspoons dried parsley

Preheat oven to 400°F. Pour oil in $2\frac{1}{2}$ quart round casserole or 13x9-inch baking dish. Combine flour, salt, pepper, and sage, on waxed paper. Coat chicken with flour mixture. Place chicken, skin side down, in baking dish and coat with the oil. Turn chicken to bake with skin side up. Do not add additional oil. Bake for 40 minutes.

While chicken is baking, prepare Yorkshire Pudding. Sift flour, baking powder, and salt into a medium bowl. Gradually beat in milk, eggs, and parsley. Remove chicken from the oven and pour pudding over chicken. Do not remove excess fat from baking dish. To catch any overflow, place the baking dish on a cookie sheet. Return to the oven for an additional 20-25 minutes or until pudding is puffed and brown.

Golden Pheasant Inn

"A bite of France in Bucks County" ~ Innkeeper

Romantic lodging is available at the 1857 fieldstone Golden Pheasant Inn. All rooms have 1850s period style decor and afford a view of the Delaware River and canal. The Golden Pheasant Inn, listed on the National Register of Historic Places, was built as a mule barge stop to service travelers on the canal.

Michel Faure, one of the region's finest chefs, presents his creative country French cuisine in three traditionally restored dining rooms. The romantic setting of the Tavern Room features a fireplace, beamed ceiling, an exposed stonewall, and a brightly colored collection of Quimper Pottery from Brittany, France. The Blaise Room offers quiet, intimate dining. The canal, which is illuminated at night, can be seen from the candlelit, converted greenhouse dining area.

"'Exquisite' is the word to describe this experience." ~Philadelphia Inquirer

INNKEEPERS:	Barbara and Michel Faure
ADDRESS:	763 River Road
	Erwinna, Pennsylvania 18920
TELEPHONE:	(610) 294-9595; (800) 830-4474
E-MAIL:	Barbara@goldenpheasant.com
WEBSITE:	www.goldenpheasant.com
ROOMS:	5 Rooms; 1 Cottage; Private baths
CHILDREN:	Age 8 and older welcome
PETS:	Welcome in the Cottage

Sautéed Chicken Breasts with Mustard Sauce

Makes 8 Servings

4	tablespoons unsalted butter
3	tablespoons oil
4	whole chicken breasts; skinless, boned and halved
3	medium shallots, finely chopped
1	cup French white wine
1½	cups chicken stock
3	medium garlic cloves, minced
1	cup heavy cream
4	tablespoons grainy mustard
2	tablespoons tarragon, freshly chopped
2	teaspoons thyme, freshly chopped

Salt
White pepper, freshly ground
½ cup flat leaf parsley, chopped

In a large skillet, heat ½ of the butter and ½ of the oil over medium high heat. Add chicken breasts and sauté until golden brown on both sides. Remove chicken and set aside. Add remaining butter and oil to the skillet; heat until foamy. Add shallots and sauté 3 minutes. Add wine, stock, and garlic. Bring to a boil and reduce heat to simmer. Simmer until liquid is reduced to 1½ cups. Whisk in cream and mustard. Bring to a boil and cook until slightly thickened. Add tarragon and thyme. Stir and season, to taste. Return chicken to skillet and cook about 5 minutes longer to heat though. Do not overcook.
Garnish with parsley and serve hot.

Grilled Pork Chops with Orange Basil Sauce

Makes 8 Servings

For Pork Chops and Marinade:

1	tablespoon orange zest
1	cup orange juice
$\frac{1}{3}$	cup olive oil
$\frac{1}{3}$	cup Worcestershire sauce
$\frac{1}{3}$	cup orange blossom honey (substitute ordinary honey)
1	tablespoon light brown sugar
$\frac{1}{2}$	teaspoon salt
$\frac{1}{4}$	teaspoon black pepper, freshly ground
8	pork loin chops, $1\frac{1}{2}$ –inches thick, with bone

For Salsa:

2	cups oranges; peeled, sectioned, and chopped
$\frac{1}{2}$	cup fresh basil
1	cup green onions, finely chopped
$\frac{1}{2}$	cup red bell pepper, chopped
$\frac{1}{2}$	teaspoon orange zest
$\frac{1}{2}$	cup avocado, peeled and chopped
$\frac{1}{2}$	tablespoon jalapeño, seeded and minced (optional)
$\frac{1}{8}$	teaspoon salt

Combine orange zest, orange juice, olive oil, Worcestershire sauce, honey, sugar, salt, and pepper in a bowl. Set aside. Place pork chops in a plastic bag in a shallow dish. Add marinade to the bag. Seal the bag and refrigerate overnight, turning the bag occasionally.

Remove the pork chops and drain marinade into a saucepan. Bring marinade to a boil and cook for 3 minutes. Cook pork chops on a medium hot grill for 3-5 minutes on each side. Brush with marinade. Reduce heat and close grill. Cook 12-15 minutes on each side, brushing with marinade several times.

For salsa, combine orange sections, basil, green onion, bell pepper, orange zest, avocado, jalapeño, and salt in a bowl. Toss to mix. To serve, spread salsa around pork chops on individual plates.

Spinach and Feta Pie

Makes 8 Servings

1	pound spinach leaves
2	tablespoons olive oil

Extra olive oil for brushing phyllo

12	spring onions, chopped
¾	pound feta cheese
4	tablespoons Italian parsley, chopped
4	tablespoons fresh dill, chopped

Pinch of nutmeg, freshly grated
Ground black pepper

12-14	phyllo sheets

Wash spinach well to remove all traces of sand. Drain well and dry thoroughly. Stem the spinach and chop into small pieces. In a large sauté pan, warm 2 tablespoons of oil over medium heat. Add the spinach and onions. Sauté until the spinach wilts and cooks down, about 5 minutes. Transfer to a sieve and drain well. Press out as much liquid as possible. Chop coarsely and set aside.

In a large bowl, mash the feta cheese with a fork. Add parsley, dill, nutmeg, and spinach mixture. Mix with fork.

Preheat oven to 350°F. Brush a 10½ x 16 x 2½- inch pan with olive oil. Place 6 phyllo sheets in the pan, lightly brushing each one with oil before adding the next. Spoon the spinach mixture on top of the layer of phyllo and spread evenly. Place 6-8 more phyllo sheets on top of the spinach mixture, brushing each one with oil before adding the next. Cover and chill for about 30 minutes. Use a sharp knife to score the top 4 sheets into large squares. Bake for 30 minutes until golden. Let rest for 10 minutes. Cut into squares and serve.

Harvest Moon

The Harvest Moon Bed and Breakfast is a turn-of-the-century guesthouse in a timeless part of the world where values and a sense of culture run deep. New Holland is a place where church bells still toll, and home-baked goods are prevalent in the area restaurants. Furniture makers, quilters crafting in differing styles, and the renowned New Holland Horse Stables are yours to discover during your sojourn.

Your hosts at the Harvest Moon are chefs. Emphasis is placed on the craft, history, and understanding of fine dining at their inn. Italian, Holiday, German, Holistic, and the ever-popular Chocolate Weekends are culinary events at the Harvest Moon. Wine and cheese tours are also on their schedule of momentous occasions. Sample the area's finest wines and visit Amish-run dairy farms with real cheese caves.

INNKEEPERS:	Carl and Marlies Kosko
ADDRESS:	311 E. Main St.
	New Holland, Pennsylvania 17557
TELEPHONE:	(717) 354-0213; (888) 824-3763
E-MAIL:	info@harvestmoonbandb.com
WEBSITE:	www.harvestmoonbandb.com
ROOMS:	4 Rooms; 4 Private baths
CHILDREN:	Welcome
PETS:	Not allowed

Turkey Scrapple

Makes 10 Servings

"This recipe is a great alternative to the traditional. It provides all of the taste with none of the "scraps". However, it will not freeze well. You have about two days to eat it all which won't be a problem."
~ Innkeeper, Harvest Moon Bed & Breakfast

2	pounds ground turkey
2	tablespoons canola oil
1	teaspoon black pepper
1½	tablespoons poultry seasoning
1	tablespoon garlic powder
2	cubes chicken bouillon
1	cup water
1	cup corn flour

Butter, to taste

In a large skillet, cook turkey and canola oil over low heat being careful not to brown. Add pepper, poultry seasoning, and garlic powder. Cook an additional 5 minutes until the turkey is cooked through and the ingredients have incorporated. Add water and bouillon cubes and bring to a boil. Add the corn flour, stirring rapidly, so that it does not stick to the pan. Remove from heat and place in a plastic lined bread loaf pan. Refrigerate overnight.

Remove from pan and slice the scrapple, as you would bread. Fry in pan with a bit of oil for about 3-5 minutes until brown. Flip and repeat on the other side. When brown, throw in a bit of butter for taste. This is a perfect brunch dish.

Hickory Bridge Farm

At the base of the foothills of the Appalachian Mountains, sits the Hickory Bridge Farm. A well-stocked trout stream winds through the farm, which is nine miles west of Gettysburg. Farm-related antiques decorate the late-1700s farmhouse, where deer can be spotted from the large deck in the backyard. Quiet country cottages are positioned in the woods by the creek. A full breakfast is featured Monday through Saturday at the farmhouse, and Continental breakfast baskets are prepared for guests on Sunday.

Since 1977, delicious, bountiful dinners have been served in the restored 180-year-old barn. Linen tablecloths are often adorned with fresh flowers from the garden. The main course of the dinner is presented family-style at your own table, and consists of three entrees, several vegetables, corn fritters, and stewed apples. There is always dessert, and the dessert is always homemade.

INNKEEPERS:	Mary Lynn and Robert Martin
ADDRESS:	96 Hickory Bridge Road
	Orrtanna, Pennsylvania 17353
TELEPHONE:	(717) 642-5261; (800) 642-1766
E-MAIL:	hickory@pa.net
WEBSITE:	www.hickorybridgefarm.com
ROOMS:	7 Rooms; 6 Private baths
CHILDREN:	Welcome; Call ahead
PETS:	Not allowed

Dutch Ham Loaf

Makes 8 Servings

½	pound ground country ham
1	pound ground smoked ham
½	pound ground pork
2	slices of bread
½	cup of milk
2	eggs, slightly beaten

Preheat oven to 325°F. Mix ground meats thoroughly. Place bread in a shallow bowl with milk just to moisten. Remove the bread, and mix with eggs. Add to the meat mixture and mold into a loaf. Place in a greased, shallow pan. Bake for 1 hour. Serve with Jezebel Sauce.

Jezebel sauce:

½	cup apple jelly
½	cup pineapple jam
2	tablespoons prepared mustard
1	tablespoon horseradish

Combine all ingredients in a saucepan and heat. Do not boil.

Serve over ham loaf.

Turkey Divan

Makes 6 Servings

1	(10-ounce) can cream of cheddar soup
1	(10-ounce) can cream of chicken soup
½	cup mayonnaise
1	teaspoon lemon juice
6	thin slices of baked ham
1	package frozen broccoli florets
2	cups turkey, chopped
2	cups Ritz crackers, crushed

Preheat oven to 350°F. Combine the first 4 ingredients and set aside. Spray cooking oil lightly on the bottom of a 9x13-inch baking dish and layer ham in the dish. Place broccoli on top of the ham and add a layer of turkey. Spoon cream mixture on top and sprinkle with crackers. Bake for 30 minutes.

Pork Chops with Scalloped Potatoes

Makes 6 Servings

3	tablespoons butter or margarine
3	tablespoons flour
$1\frac{1}{2}$	teaspoons salt
$\frac{1}{4}$	teaspoon pepper
1	($14\frac{1}{2}$-ounce) can chicken broth
6	rib or loin pork chops (3/4-inch thick)
2	tablespoons cooking oil
6	cups potatoes, peeled and thinly sliced
1	medium onion, sliced

Paprika and chopped fresh parsley (optional)

Melt butter in a saucepan. Stir in flour, salt, and pepper. Add chicken broth and cook, stirring constantly until the mixture boils. Cook for 1 minute. Remove from heat and set aside. In a skillet, brown pork chops in oil. Season the pork chops, to taste, with additional salt and pepper. Layer the potatoes and onion in a greased, 13x9x2-inch baking dish. Pour the broth mixture over potatoes and place the pork chops on top.

Cover and bake for 1 hour. Uncover and bake an additional 30 minutes or until potatoes are tender. Sprinkle with paprika and parsley.

The Brafferton Inn

Filled with a mix of history, culture, and art, The Brafferton is the oldest continual residence in Gettysburg. Built in 1786, using brown stone native to the area, the three historic homes that comprise the Brafferton Inn are in the center of town, one-half block from Lincoln Square.

In July of 1863, the town of Gettysburg exploded in civil conflict. As Union troops passed the stone house on York Street, a Confederate sniper's bullet shattered the glass in an upstairs window and lodged in the mantel above the fireplace, where it remains today. For months after the battle, the house served as a Catholic chapel since the church was filled with wounded soldiers. The Brafferton Inn remains a sanctuary to this day.

A mural, encompassing all four walls in the dining room, is a conversational springboard for guests during breakfast at The Brafferton. Virginia Jacobs Mclaughlin, nationally recognized American primitive folk artist, painted this visual history lesson.

INNKEEPERS:	Joan, Brian, and Amybeth Hodges
ADDRESS:	44 York Street
	Gettysburg, Pennsylvania 17325
TELEPHONE:	(717) 337-3423; (866) 337-3423
E-MAIL:	innkeepers@brafferton.com
WEBSITE:	www.brafferton.com
ROOMS:	18 Rooms; 6 Suites; Private baths
CHILDREN:	Age 10 and older welcome
PETS:	Not allowed

Crab and Asparagus Quiche

Makes 6 Servings

1	**9-inch round pastry pie shell, unbaked**
$\frac{1}{2}$	**medium onion, diced**
$\frac{1}{2}$	**pound thin asparagus, sliced into $\frac{1}{2}$-inch pieces**
1	**tablespoon unsalted butter**
6	**eggs**
$\frac{1}{2}$	**cup milk**
4	**ounces cheddar cheese, grated**
$\frac{1}{4}$	**cup red pepper, diced**
1	**scallion, thinly sliced**
1	**teaspoon salt**
$\frac{1}{4}$	**teaspoon thyme**
$\frac{1}{8}$	**teaspoon black pepper**

Pinch nutmeg
4 ounces crab meat

Preheat oven to 350°F. In a skillet, Sauté onions and asparagus in a tablespoon of unsalted butter until softened. Set aside to cool. Combine eggs, milk, cheese, red pepper, scallions, and seasonings in a large bowl. Stir until well combined. Add cooled onion and asparagus mixture. Pour into pie shell. Bake for 1 hour. Cool quiche for 10 minutes before serving.

Greystone Manor

The quiet charm of the Greystone Manor is evident as soon as you enter the Victorian lobby. Leaded, beveled glass doors, and plaster-cast wall and ceiling sculptures add to the warm and cozy feeling of the inn. Set on top of a hill on two acres, this brick mansion is in the heart of Amish Country. The Greystone Manor was constructed in 1883 from a farmhouse built in the mid-1800s. Originally a barn, the Carriage House is guest-ready with pleasing country decor. Amenities include numerous patios, outdoor pool and hot tub, gardens, and ponds. Consider taking a buggy ride, visiting an Amish homestead, attending a performance at the Amish Experience Theatre, or touring the Americana Museum while staying in the village of Bird-In-Hand.

INNKEEPERS:	Angela and Wade Skiadas
ADDRESS:	2658 Old Philadelphia Pike
	Bird-in-Hand, Pennsylvania 17505
TELEPHONE:	(717) 393-4233
E-MAIL:	angela@greystonemanor.com
WEBSITE:	www.greystonemanor.com
ROOMS:	6 Rooms; 4 Suites; Private baths
CHILDREN:	Welcome
PETS:	Welcome; Resident dog

Greek Quiche

Makes 6 Servings

"This is adapted from my Greek background." ~ Innkeeper, Greystone Manor

1	9-inch round pastry pie shell, unbaked
6	extra large eggs
1	teaspoon butter or olive oil
¼	cup onions, chopped

Dash of pepper
Pinch of salt

⅛	teaspoon oregano
⅛	teaspoon basil
½	cup frozen spinach (thawed, with excess water squeezed out and patted dry)
½	cup feta cheese, crumbled
¼	cup diced tomatoes
½	teaspoon paprika

Preheat oven to 350°F. Beat eggs in mixing bowl. Set aside. Cook onions and butter in a pan until translucent. Add pepper, salt, oregano, and basil; mix. Let cool. Layer spinach, feta cheese, tomatoes, and onion mixture in the pie shell. Pour beaten eggs over layers in the pie shell and top with paprika.

Bake 45 minutes to 1 hour until firm. Let stand 10 minutes before serving.

Fruit Specialties

Fruit

Specialties

Buhl Mansion Guesthouse & Spa

One of America's most luxurious bed and breakfasts, Buhl Mansion is listed on the National Register of Historic Places. This 1890s castle offers 10 opulent guestrooms with fireplaces, Jacuzzi's, the finest amenities, and royal service.

The grand, oak staircase that ascends to the second and third floors is used to reach the guest rooms. A hand-painted mural of formal gardens and cherubs welcomes you on the third level. Buhl Mansion is home to a splendid art gallery of original oil paintings, bronze statuary, and magnificent antiques. The full-service spa, with nearly 100 indulgent spa treatments available, provides the ultimate in luxury and pampering. The Buhl Mansion is perfect for romantic getaways and executive retreats. The Victorian greenhouse, carriage house, and formal gardens provide a truly memorable backdrop for castle weddings.

INNKEEPERS:	Donna and Jim Winner
ADDRESS:	422 East State Street
	Sharon, Pennsylvania 16146
TELEPHONE:	(724) 346-3046; (866) 345-2845
E-MAIL:	info@buhlmansion.com
WEBSITE:	www.buhlmansion.com
ROOMS:	10 Rooms; Private baths
CHILDREN:	Age 12 and older welcome
PETS:	Not allowed

Buhl Castle Champagne Punch

Makes 30 Servings

"This recipe was created for a summer garden party.
The taste-testing 'till perfection was great fun!"
~Innkeeper, Buhl Mansion Guesthouse and Spa

4	**bottles of champagne**
4	**cups orange juice**
4	**cups pineapple juice**
2	**cups lemon/lime juice**
1	**cup Grenadine**
2	**cups Chambord liquor**

**Lemons, limes, or oranges, thinly sliced; and/or raspberries
and strawberries, whole, for garnish**

Combine all ingredients in a large punch bowl.

Garnish with fresh fruit of your choice: thinly sliced lemons, limes, oranges; and/or whole raspberries, and strawberries.

Locust Brook Lodge

The Locust Brook Lodge incorporates new, clean, construction with rustic ambiance. On a one-hundred-acre farm in the town of Butler, the natural wooded garden at the lodge is home to deer and other furry friends. The Trout Room will appeal to the fisherman, from the earthtone colors to the fishing memorabilia displayed on the walls. The soft southwest colors show off the collection of pottery displayed in the Native American Room. Stabling for your horse is available at the Locust Brook Lodge. Farm-fresh ingredients and home-baked bread are standard breakfast staples. Afternoon milk and cookies are a special treat.

"...You are safe and secure in a big house in the woods.
Think 'Big Chill' in terms of re-uniting with family or friends." ~ Guest

INNKEEPERS:	Carol and Ed Pawlowicz
ADDRESS:	179 Eagle Mill Road
	Butler, Pennsylvania 16001
TELEPHONE:	(724) 283-8453
E-MAIL:	locustbrooklodge@earthlink.net
WEBSITE:	home.earthlink.net/~locustbrooklodge/
ROOMS:	7 Rooms; Private baths
CHILDREN:	Welcome
PETS:	Dogs and Cats welcome

Ginger Orange Slices

Makes 6 Servings

3	navel oranges
1	tablespoon crystallized ginger, finely chopped
½	cup orange juice
2	tablespoons brown sugar
½	teaspoon rum flavoring
½	teaspoon vanilla extract
4	tablespoons dried cranberries, for garnish

Slice off both ends of one orange. Stand orange on end and cut away peel and pith. Slice into 1/4-inch slices. Repeat with remaining oranges. Sprinkle the ginger on the bottom of a 9-inch glass pie plate. Arrange the oranges in a spiral pattern, overlapping slightly. Set aside.

Combine orange juice and brown sugar in a small non-reactive sauce pan. Boil 5 minutes over medium high heat. Remove from heat and cool slightly. Combine rum flavoring and vanilla extract; pour over oranges. Chill thoroughly.

Invert a serving plate over pie plate, quickly turn both over, and lift away pie plate. Sprinkle with dried cranberries and serve at once.

The Boothby Inn

"I have stayed at B & B's, small inns and guest houses from coast to coast and continent to continent, I have never described one as perfect ~ until now. Congratulations! Beauty, utility, and amenities coupled with hospitality to make this that stay one searches for." ~ Guest

When you open the front door, you enter into a spectacular hall with the original wood stairway and stained glass windows. Expect a warm greeting, sounds of classical music, fires in the fireplaces, and pampering in the wondrous guest rooms. The accommodations at The Boothby Inn are professionally decorated with an international theme. Would you prefer the France, Japan, Scotland, or Africa Room? On warm mornings, breakfast may be served on the garden patio. Savor the most luxurious accommodations in downtown Erie and count on a very memorable stay.

INNKEEPERS:	Gloria Knox
ADDRESS:	311 West Sixth Street
	Erie, Pennsylvania 16507
TELEPHONE:	(814) 456-1888; (866) 266-8429
E-MAIL:	info@theboothbyinn.com
WEBSITE:	www.theboothbyinn.com
ROOMS:	4 Rooms; Private baths
CHILDREN:	Age 12 and older welcome
PETS:	Not allowed

Dreamsicle Oranges

Makes 12 Servings

"Imagine...this easy! Everyone always asks, what is the sauce?"
~ Innkeeper, Boothby Inn

2	cups water
2	cups of sugar
6	oranges
6	teaspoons orange zest
2	teaspoons vanilla

Bring the water to a boil. Stir in sugar, and boil 5 minutes. Add orange zest and 2 teaspoons of vanilla. Boil another 5 minutes. Cool in refrigerator. Peel and slice oranges horizontally and place in a flat bowl. Pour sugar water on top.

House at the End of the Road

The House at the End of the Road is a pre-1900 farmhouse tucked away from time and traffic on twenty-five wooded acres in the western Pennsylvania town of Summerville. The Inn's Willow Bedroom looks out on the 100-year-old willow tree and the original post-and-beam barn. Bring your fly-fishing gear and try your luck in the Redbank Creek, or simply take a walk along its banks. Play target golf, horseshoes, or take advantage of the 30-foot-by-60-foot athletic court to practice your jump shot or volleyball serve.

The 8,500-acre Cook Park National Forest is nearby. The area is famous for its old growth forest, once referred to as the "Black Forest." Cook Park's "Forest Cathedral" of magnificent lofty hemlocks and white pines is a National Natural Landmark. Along the eastern border of the park, canoeing and rafting on the Clarion River is a favorite pastime.

INNKEEPERS:	Pam and David Henderson
ADDRESS:	518 Bauer Road
	Summerville, Pennsylvania 15864
TELEPHONE:	(814) 856-3480; (800) 905-6647
E-MAIL:	info@thehouseattheendoftheroad.com
WEBSITE:	www.houseattheendoftheroad.com
ROOMS:	2 Suites; Private baths
CHILDREN:	Unable to accommodate
PETS:	Not allowed

Hot Fruit Compote

Makes 12 to 15 Servings

"For a side dish or dessert" ~ Innkeeper, House at the End of the Road

1	**(14-16-ounce) can peaches, drained**
1	**(14-16-ounce) can pears, drained**
1	**(14-16-ounce) can apricots, drained**
½	**(14-16-ounce) can cherry pie filling**
½	**cup golden raisins**
A few drops of almond extract	
1	**cup pecans or walnuts, toasted, for topping**

Preheat oven to 325°F. Combine all ingredients until well blended. Pour into a greased 13x9-inch casserole dish. Bake for 20-30 minutes until bubbly and heated through. Don't overcook. Sprinkle with toasted pecans or walnuts.

Apple Bin Inn

APPLE BIN INN
Bed & Breakfast

At the Apple Bin Inn, the proximity of the Amish neighbors provides a daily reminder to slow down and focus on the simpler things in life.

As you turn into the driveway, you'll be welcomed by an acre of park-like tranquility. Enter the main house as friends do, through the back door, and into the kitchen with an arched-brick hearth. The country dining room has the original wide-plank flooring and is the staging area for the scrumptious breakfast that will await you each morning. The comfortable living room features an extensive library to suit all reading tastes, along with comfy sofas and chairs for reading, knitting, games, or just talking with newfound friends. Once settled into a beautiful guest room, suite, or cottage, you'll know that the Apple Bin Inn combines the best of both worlds. Snuggle up under an antique family heirloom quilt and check the e-mail messages on your laptop computer using the inn's free wireless Internet access. During the summer months, the in-ground swimming pool will beckon you to take time to refresh and re-energize.

INNKEEPERS:	Steve and Jamie Shane
ADDRESS:	2835 Willow Street Pike
	Willow Street, Pennsylvania (Lancaster County) 17584
TELEPHONE:	(717) 464-5881; (800) 338-4296
E-MAIL:	stay@applebininn.com
WEBSITE:	www.applebininn.com
ROOMS:	5 Rooms; 2 Suites; 1 Cottage; Private baths
CHILDREN:	Welcome
PETS:	Not allowed; Resident cats

Pecan Baked Apples

Makes 4 Servings

"An impressive fruit dish, perfect on cold mornings or anytime you want to pamper your guests!" ~ Innkeeper, Apple Bin Inn

Apples:

4	Rome apples of equal size (Stayman or Cortland apples also work well. Red Delicious apples do not work.)
½	stick, unsalted butter
2	tablespoons cinnamon
2	tablespoons light brown sugar

Topping:

½	cup light brown sugar
20	pecan halves, chopped
4	teaspoons raisins
1	teaspoon cinnamon

Dash of pumpkin pie spice

Heavy whipping cream, for topping

For the apples: Core and peel apples, leaving a ring of skin around bottom third of each apple. Cut a small slice off bottoms of apples (so they don't roll) and place in a glass baking dish. Into each core cavity, put a pat of butter, a dash of cinnamon, and a dash of brown sugar. Cover baking dish with plastic wrap, and poke a few holes in the plastic wrap to allow air to escape. Microwave apples on high for 2 minutes; baste apples with juices from glass baking dish. Microwave on high for 1 more minute, or until apples are desired softness (poke with fork to test).

For the topping: Combine topping ingredients in a glass mixing bowl. Add some of the juices from the apple baking dish. Microwave on high for 30-45 seconds and then stir well (topping should be thick and syrupy).

To serve: Place apples in dessert bowls. Spoon a generous amount of topping over each apple. Fill each apple core cavity with heavy whipping cream. Serve hot.

Flowers & Thyme

All variations of the colors lavender and pink enhance the acre of countryside that is home to Flowers & Thyme. From early spring until late fall, perennial flowers mixed with annuals, plus the herb gardens create a colorful and lush vision for guests of the inn. "We've been featured in the *Birds & Blooms* magazine, but it's the thoughtful comments from our guests that we cherish the most," say the innkeepers.

Built in 1941, the brick Colonial house was constructed by an Amish man for a Mennonite family. Cheery, eclectic furnishings lend an air of elegant simplicity to Flowers & Thyme. The large, commodious Gathering Room has a vaulted ceiling and an expanse of windows overlooking a peaceful valley with a working farm. Bountiful breakfasts are served in this room.
Aromas from snow pea garden breakfast quiche, French toast with southern fried apples, or eggs scrambled with a rich chicken sauce may be wafting through the inn as you awaken.

INNKEEPERS:	Don and Ruth Harnish
ADDRESS:	238 Strasburg Pike
	Lancaster, Pennsylvania 17602
TELEPHONE:	(717) 393-1460
E-MAIL:	Innkeeper@flowersandthyme.com
WEBSITE:	www.flowersandthyme.com
ROOMS:	3 Rooms; Private baths
CHILDREN:	Age 12 and older welcome
PETS:	Not allowed

Pear Streusel

Makes 6 Servings

Adapted from Blooming Glen Church

For the pears:
6	cups pears, sliced and peeled
1/4	cup sugar
2	tablespoons flour
1/2	teaspoon nutmeg
1/2	teaspoon cinnamon

For the streusel:
1/2	cup old-fashioned rolled oats
3	tablespoons butter
2	tablespoons flour
2	tablespoons brown sugar

For the pears: Preheat oven to 425°F. Combine pears, sugar, flour, nutmeg, and cinnamon; pour into a casserole dish.

For the streusel: Combine oats, butter, flour and brown sugar; sprinkle over pear mixture. Bake for 45-50 minutes.

Campbell House

An 1868 city cottage, situated in the Laurel Highlands, is home to the Campbell House Bed and Breakfast. The inn is an adult getaway in the town of Ligonier. It is located on the Lincoln Highway Heritage Corridor, the first transcontinental highway in the United States. The roadway was completed in 1925, to become Route 30. Ligonier is the site for the new Lincoln Highway Welcome Center/Experience, which will house the area's historical archives and a gift shop.

Fort Ligonier, a full-scale reconstruction of the 1758–1766 original fort, is a favored daytime destination for guests of the Campbell House. This colonial fortress protected the essential land route to Pittsburgh and the western frontier beyond. Living history reenactments, battles, encampments, folk crafts, and archaeological digs will augment your educational tour with an intensity no classroom experience can replicate.

INNKEEPERS:	Patti Campbell
ADDRESS:	305 East Main Street
	Ligonier, Pennsylvania 15658
TELEPHONE:	(724) 238-9812; (888) 238-9812
E-MAIL:	innkeeper@campbellhousebnb.com
WEBSITE:	www.soupkid.com
ROOMS:	4 Rooms; 2 Suites; Private baths
CHILDREN:	Unable to accommodate
PETS:	Not allowed

Roasted Pears with Cherry Maraschino Craisins

Makes 8 Servings

"This recipe is tasty and well-loved by Campbell House guests.
~ Innkeeper, Campbell House Bed & Breakfast

4	**pears, D'Anjou or Bosc**
4	**tablespoons butter**
¼	**cup light brown sugar**
½	**cup cherry-flavored craisins**
⅓	**cup Maraschino cherry syrup**

Cooking spray

Preheat oven to 400°F. Steam whole pears until semi-soft. Cool. Cut pears in half. Scoop out the cores to create a cavity in each pear. Carve a thin slice from the bottom of each pear. Use a glass baking dish large enough to hold 8 pear halves in a single layer. Spray baking dish with cooking spray. Melt butter and pour into bottom of dish; sprinkle brown sugar over the melted butter. Place a single layer of pear halves in the dish. Fill each pear cavity with cherry-flavored craisins. Drizzle Maraschino syrup over the pears.

Bake uncovered. Baste with liquid from the baking dish after 20 minutes. Bake another 10 minutes until pear halves are tender. Let cool slightly. Drizzle remaining liquid from the baking dish over top of pears.

Serve in small fruit dish.

Elver Valley Farm

Rolling dairy farmland and woodland provide the natural environment for the Elver Valley Farm ranch-style Guest Home and Acorn Rock Cabin. Streams and greenery are plentiful in this area between Brandywine Valley and the Lancaster County Dutch Country. From the breakfast table, a dozen different varieties of birds may be observed. Chester County mushrooms can be requested as a part of a full breakfast.

Walk down the winding driveway to Acorn Rock Cabin, and you'll pass the children's swing and slide playground. The cabin overlooks a half-acre pond alive with frogs and fish. You are welcome to take a swim or row out in the boat and go fishing. Picnic tables are conveniently located for a meal outside. A pasture with assorted farm animals to feed and pet are in full view of the cabin.

INNKEEPERS:	Elvin and Vera Rohrer
ADDRESS:	432 Sawmill Road
	Cochranville, Pennsylvania 19330
TELEPHONE:	(717) 529-2803; (877) 863-5837
E-MAIL:	evrohrer@webtv.net
WEBSITE:	www.pafarmstay.com/elvervalley
ROOMS:	2 Rooms; 1 Cottage; Private baths
CHILDREN:	Welcome
PETS:	Not allowed

Fruit Medley

Makes 4 to 6 Servings

"This is a lovely blend of fresh fruits to serve as an appetizer for breakfast."
~ Innkeeper, Elver Valley Farm

¼	cup honey
¼	cup limeade concentrate
1	cup fresh strawberries, halved
1	cup fresh pineapple, cubed
1	cup fresh blueberries
1	cup seedless watermelon, cubed
¼	cup slivered almonds, toasted

Combine honey and limeade concentrate in a small bowl. Set aside. In a large bowl, combine all fruit. Drizzle honey/limeade dressing over fruit, tossing gently to coat. Sprinkle with almonds.

Rocky Springs

On seventeen acres along the Conestoga River, called Rocky Springs Park, sits a restored mansion house dating back to the mid-1800s. Extravagant five-course breakfasts are served to the travelers who have chosen to be overnight guests in this pre-Victorian home, now known as Rocky Springs Bed and Breakfast. Each guest room has a commanding view of the park, formerly an amusement park that was in its heyday during the early 1900s. The deck adjacent to the dining room is made of wood from the old roller coaster.

Lancaster County Central Park is within walking distance from Rocky Springs. Here are just a few of the features to explore in this park's 544 acres: a public swimming pool; skate park; innumerable trails for hiking, biking, and cross-country skiing; Historic Rockford Plantation; a Revolutionary War–era house museum; an environmental library; The Garden of Five Senses. Tree-to-tasting maple sugar events are held each spring.

INNKEEPERS:	Glori and Nevin Brubaker
ADDRESS:	1441 Millport Road
	Lancaster, Pennsylvania 17602
TELEPHONE:	(717) 509-6800; (866) 611-4647
E-MAIL:	innkeeper@rockyspringsbnb.com
WEBSITE:	www.rockyspringsbnb.com
ROOMS:	4 Rooms; 1 Cottage; Private baths
CHILDREN:	Age 12 and older welcome
PETS:	Not allowed; Resident cat

Fresh Lemon Ice

Makes 1 Pint

"This is a sweet and perfectly vibrant palate cleanser or weightless ending to a rich meal." ~ Innkeeper, Rocky Springs Bed & Breakfast

2	**lemons, plus tiny lemon wedges, for garnish**
¾	**cup sugar**
1	**cup hot water**

Baby mint sprigs, for garnish.

Wash and thinly slice lemons. Put sugar in a small bowl and top with lemon slices. Gently knead with hands for 1 minute. Do not use a wooden mallet as too much crushing will extract bitter oils from lemon rind. Pour hot water over lemon slices; stir until sugar is dissolved. Pour through sieve into a freezable container and freeze.

To serve: Sugar the rims of sherbet goblets or tiny footed glasses and place in the freezer to chill. Remove lemon ice from freezer and thaw at room temperature for 5-10 minutes. Use a mini ice cream scoop or a melon baller to scrape ice into cute little balls; place in iced goblets and garnish with a tiny fresh lemon wedge and a baby mint sprig. Refreshing!

Pineapple Hill

*"In the 1700s, it was customary to place a pineapple on your front porch
as a way of letting friends and neighbors know you were welcoming guests.
We continue this tradition by offering the same hospitality to our guests.
We hope you'll always feel welcome at Pineapple Hill." ~Innkeeper*

The Pineapple Hill Bed and Breakfast Lodging rests between New Hope's center and Washington Crossing Park. Set on almost six acres, this Colonial manor house in Buck's County was built in 1790, and has 18-inch thick walls. On the grounds, the walls of the stone barn enclose a beautifully hand-tiled pool. The rose garden is situated where the springhouse once stood. The outdoor sitting area is surrounded by the ruins of the original summer kitchen.

"Your beautiful Pineapple Hill is a Bed & Breakfast dream!" ~ *Guest*

"Thanks for letting us share your little Eden." ~ *Guest*

INNKEEPERS:	Kathryn and Charles Triolo
ADDRESS:	1324 River Road
	New Hope, Pennsylvania 18938
TELEPHONE:	(215) 862-1790
E-MAIL:	innkeeper@pineapplehill.com
WEBSITE:	www.pineapplehill.com
ROOMS:	5 Rooms; 3 Suites; 1 Cottage; Private baths
CHILDREN:	Age 12 and older welcome
PETS:	Not allowed

Baked Bananas

Makes 6 Servings

"This is wonderful as a breakfast or brunch appetizer. It also makes a great dessert." ~ Innkeeper, Pineapple Hill B&B Lodging

½	cup butter, melted
3	tablespoons fresh lemon juice
6	firm ripe bananas, peeled
⅓	cup brown sugar
1	teaspoon ground ginger
1	cup coconut, grated
½	cup heavy whipping cream, for topping

Preheat oven to 375°F. Spread melted butter and lemon juice over the bottom of a baking dish. Put bananas in the dish and coat with butter/lemon juice mixture. Mix brown sugar and ginger in a small bowl; set aside ½ of this mixture. Spread ½ of the sugar mixture over bananas. Bake for 10 minutes. Roll bananas over and pour the rest of the sugar mixture over bananas. Bake for another 5 minutes. Spread coconut over the bananas and bake for 5 more minutes.

Serve in fruit dishes. Pour heavy whipping cream over each serving.

Dillweed

D illweed Bed and Breakfast is a turn-of-the-century home built by the Dill family, early settlers of Dilltown. Antique hats, hatpins, vintage clothing, and antique toys are all part of the decor in the four guestrooms and the Garden Suite. The rooms have the charming names of Parsley, Sage, Rosemary, and Thyme. The Parsley Room has a particularly good view of Dillweed's herb garden. The on-site Trailside Shop offers two floors of country gifts and antiques for your browsing pleasure.

Dillweed is located at the beginning of Ghost Town Trail, an historic rail-trail project. The limestone-surfaced trail passes by once-thriving mining communities, following Blacklick Creek. The Ghost Town Trail is a multi-use recreational trail appropriate for hiking, biking, horseback riding, and cross-country skiing.

INNKEEPERS:	Corey, Kyra and Cindy Gilmore
ADDRESS:	PO Box 1
	Dilltown, Pennsylvania 15929
TELEPHONE:	(814) 446-6465
E-MAIL:	dillweed@floodcity.net
WEBSITE:	www.dillweedinc.com
ROOMS:	4 Rooms; 1 Suite; Private and shared baths
CHILDREN:	Welcome
PETS:	Not allowed

Grapes in Rosemary Syrup

Makes 4 Servings

"Syrup may be used over melons and other fresh fruits."
~ Innkeeper, Dillweed Bed & Breakfast

$\frac{1}{3}$	cup sugar
$\frac{1}{3}$	cup white wine
2	tablespoons water
1	tablespoon rosemary, finely chopped
1	tablespoon lime juice
$\frac{1}{2}$	pound seedless grapes, white or red

Syrup:

$\frac{1}{4}$	cup sour cream for topping
4	sprigs of rosemary, for garnish

In saucepan, bring sugar, wine, and water to a boil. Reduce heat, and add chopped rosemary. Simmer for 10 minutes. Remove from heat. Add lime juice. Refrigerate until ready to use.

To serve: Remove stems from seedless white or red grapes. Toss grapes with syrup. Divide and place grapes in 4 stemmed glasses. Top with a dollop of sour cream and a sprig of rosemary.

Morgan Century Farm

Established in 1850 as a family farm, the original farmhouse, one barn, and two outbuildings still remain on the Morgan Century Farm grounds. A small milk house built in the 1930s now serves as a potting shed. In 1995, great-great granddaughter, Linda Faye Morgan, and her husband Ken Florentine began a three-year restoration of the main building as a country inn. Being antique car lovers, with a special interest in Plymouths, Ken and Linda named each guest room in the main house after a Plymouth model of the early 1950s. A rustic two-story cottage, meant just for two, is another lodging choice at Morgan Century Farm. Or, you may want to consider the old barn hayloft with its deck extending out above Elks Creek. The Elegant Duck Gift Shop is located in the lower part of the barn.

Each morning, a three-course breakfast is served, with complimentary wine and cheese offered in the afternoon.

INNKEEPERS:	Ken and Linda Florentine
ADDRESS:	Route 1 Lincoln Falls
	Forksville, Pennsylvania 18616
TELEPHONE:	(570) 924-4909; (888) 335-1583
E-MAIL:	morcenfm@epix.net
WEBSITE:	www.pa-bedandbreakfast.com
ROOMS:	5 Rooms; 1 Cottage; Private baths
CHILDREN:	Unable to accommodate
PETS:	Welcome in the cottage; Resident cat

G.W.'s Applesauce

Makes 6 to 8 Servings

"A great compliment to any meal."
~ Innkeeper, Morgan Century Farm Bed & Breakfast

6-8	medium apples, any variety
1	(16-ounce) jar chunky applesauce
½	cup seedless raisins (golden are best)
¼	teaspoon rum extract

Wash and core apples. Cut into chunks, leaving the skin on. Place in saucepan with ¼ cup water. Cover and heat to boiling. Reduce heat and simmer, stirring occasionally to break up apples. Cook until tender, about 10-20 minutes. Mash the apples. Add applesauce, raisins, and rum extract to apples in saucepan. Cover and heat for 10 more minutes. Remove from heat. Chill and serve.

Terra Nova House

Innkeepers Barry and Sandy Miller were both born and raised in Easton. When their second careers ended, they began the search for their first bed and breakfast. They discovered their perfect 1901 Victorian in Mercer County's Grove City, and called it Terra Nova House. The other permanent residents of the home are: Jada, a precocious Silver Back Persian, who will tug at your heartstrings with a single look; and Molly, the lovable Golden Retriever who will always want to give you her favorite toy. A hand-painted ocean mural graces the walls of the Caribbean Room, one of five guestrooms. The British Empire Room's deep red tones capture the flavor of English royalty. Tasty home-cooked breakfasts are presented in the airy and intimate dining room. China cupboards and a corner fireplace complete the cozy feel of this room.

INNKEEPERS:	Barry and Sandy Miller
ADDRESS:	322 West Poplar Street
	Grove City, Pennsylvania 16127
TELEPHONE:	(724) 450-0712; (877) 837-6682
E-MAIL:	info@terranovahouse.com
WEBSITE:	www.terranovahouse.com
ROOMS:	4 Rooms; 1 Suites; Private baths
CHILDREN:	Age 12 and older welcome
PETS:	Not allowed

Hawaiian Cream Fruit Salad

Makes 8 to 10 Servings

"I make this the night before and let the flavors blend and the pudding mix thicken. Also, I don't add the banana until just before I serve it."
~ *Innkeeper, Terra Nova House Bed & Breakfast*

1	(20-ounce) can pineapple tidbits
1	(11-ounce) can mandarin orange segments
1	(16-ounce) can peach slices
1	(16-ounce) can pear slices
1	apple
1	banana
1	(3.4-ounce) package vanilla instant pudding mix
1½	cups milk
2	ounces frozen orange juice concentrate
¾	cup sour cream

Drain all canned fruit. Cut canned fruit and fresh fruit into bite-sized pieces and place in a large bowl. Set aside. In a small bowl, combine pudding mix, milk, and orange juice concentrate. Beat for 2 minutes. Add sour cream and mix thoroughly. Pour pudding mixture over fruit and stir to coat. Cover and refrigerate at least 2 hours.

Reynolds Mansion

Linn Street
Bellefonte, Pennsylvania

A s you pass through the iron gates, the 1885 Reynolds Mansion reveals its blend of Gothic, Italianate, and Queen Anne styles of architecture.

Enter the grand foyer and you'll see Eastlake woodwork, stained-glass windows, a brass candelabra, and a fireplace. The Victorians always did want to make a good first impression. The main staircase is hand-carved walnut with an ornate newel post and gas lamp. Three stained-glass windows illuminate the rich architectural details along the way. Grace's Garden Room was featured on the cover of *Country Victorian* magazine, showing its inlaid wood floor and sitting area in the turret. A ceiling mural of cherubs is the highlight of Louisa's Cherub Room. A full breakfast is served at the civilized hour of 9:00 A.M. Afterwards, take your coffee to the Snuggery and peruse the morning newspaper.

INNKEEPERS:	Joseph P. Heidt III, Joseph P. Heidt, Jr., and Charlotte Heidt
ADDRESS:	101 W. Linn Street
	Bellefonte, Pennsylvania 16823
TELEPHONE:	(814) 353-8407; (800) 899-3929
E-MAIL:	innkeeper@reynoldsmansion.com
WEBSITE:	www.reynoldsmansion.com
ROOMS:	6 Rooms; Private baths
CHILDREN:	Age 12 and older welcome
PETS:	Call ahead; Resident dogs and cat

Heavenly Peaches

Serves 1 Peach per Person

Adapted from *Angel of the Sea B&B Cookbook*

"This dish is served warm." ~ Innkeeper, Reynolds Mansion Bed & Breakfast

½	cup brown sugar, divided
¼	cup oatmeal
¼	cup pecans, chopped
¼	cup granola
Handful of raisins	
¼	cup butter, melted
1	(20-ounce) can peach haves, drained
½	cup vanilla yogurt, for topping

Prepare topping by combining ¼ cup of the brown sugar, oatmeal, pecans, granola, raisins, and melted butter. Mix well and set aside. Arrange a single layer of peach halves, rounded sides down, in a shallow baking dish. Place ¼ teaspoon of the remaining brown sugar in the center of each peach.

Broil peaches for 5 minutes or until all the brown sugar has melted and been absorbed by the peaches. Remove from broiler and place heaping spoonfuls of the topping in the center of each peach. (It helps to mold topping with your hands.) Place under broiler again for approximately 1-2 minutes just before serving, being very careful not to burn. Remove from broiler, and top each peach with a tablespoon of vanilla yogurt.

Desserts

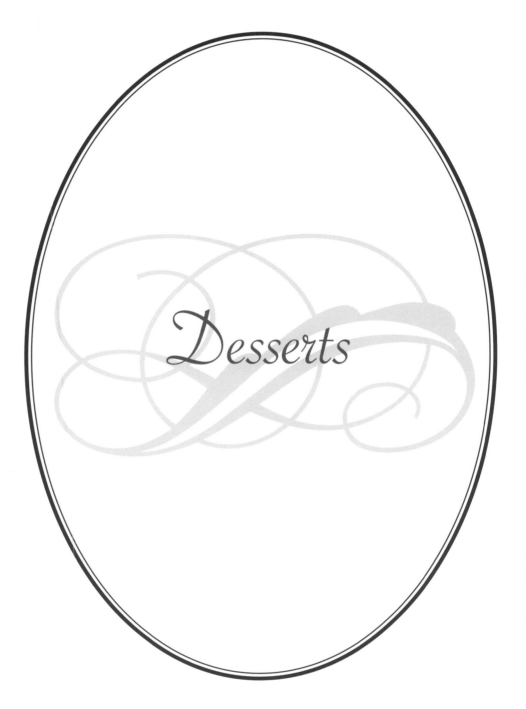

Desserts

New Hope's 1870 Wedgwood Inn

This Wedgwood-blue Victorian "Painted Lady" is listed on Bucks County Registry of Historic Places. Wedgwood Inn is spelled Wedgwood, not "Wedgewood," because Wedgwood Inn is named after the Englishman, Josiah Wedgwood, who invented the famous Wedgwood-blue bone china. The original portion of the inn served as a campsite for General George Washington and 1,200 Continental Army soldiers in December of 1776, prior to the famous Christmas Eve crossing of the Delaware River.

The inn is located on two private acres in a park-like setting, with flower-lined brick walkways leading to two gazebos and a hammock. New Hope's Historic Village is just steps away. Breakfast is served daily—in bed, on the expansive dining porch, or on one of the Victorian-style covered porches. Homemade goodies are available all day long.

INNKEEPERS:	Carl & Nadine Glassman
ADDRESS:	111 West Bridge Street
	New Hope Historic District, Pennsylvania 18938
TELEPHONE:	(215) 862-2570
E-MAIL:	stay@wedgwoodinn.com
WEBSITE:	www.wedgwoodinn.com
ROOMS:	7 Rooms; 1 Suite; 1 Cottage
CHILDREN:	Age 12 and older welcome
PETS:	Not allowed

Wedgwood Sunflower Cookies

Makes 3 Dozen Cookies

"You may substitute chocolate chips or raisins for the coconut, or try all of the ingredients together!" ~ Innkeeper, New Hope's 1870 Wedgwood Inn

1	cup sunflower margarine
1	cup sugar
1	cup brown sugar, packed
2	eggs
1	teaspoon vanilla
2	cups flour
1	teaspoon baking soda
$\frac{1}{2}$	teaspoon baking powder
$\frac{1}{4}$	teaspoon salt
2	cups rolled oats
1	cup flaked coconut
1	cup sunflower kernels, raw or roasted

Preheat oven to 350°F. In a medium mixing bowl, combine margarine and sugars until well blended. Add eggs and vanilla. Stir the flour, baking soda, baking powder, and salt; mix well. Add to the margarine mixture. Stir in oats, coconut, and sunflower kernels. Drop by rounded tablespoons onto ungreased baking sheet. Bake cookies for 8-10 minutes or until brown around the edges.

Country Farmhouse

S et the mood for a peaceful stay by playing soft music on the 1860s pump organ in the parlor of the 1834 stone Country Farmhouse. Fresh flowers, a handmade Amish quilt on your bed, and soap - homemade by the innkeeper - will be waiting for you in your room. Wake to the smell of fresh-ground coffee. The Country Farmhouse has their own house blend that is roasted especially for their guests.

The old summer kitchen has been restored and reborn as a romantic cottage with a walk-in fireplace and a whirlpool tub. Walk through the winding paths of the cottage garden, and delight your senses with its many specimens of hollyhocks, dahlias, gladiolas, hibiscus, and roses. The comfortable tree swing is a great place for bird watching. Right around the corner, there is a walking trail that meanders along a trout preservation stream. What a wonderful place to view the swaying corn and wheat fields, or to befriend the neighboring cows.

INNKEEPERS:	Barb and Terry Stephens
ADDRESS:	1780 Donegal Springs Road
	Mount Joy, Pennsylvania 17552
TELEPHONE:	(717) 653-0935; (866) 653-0935
E-MAIL:	brguest@countryfarmhouse.net
WEBSITE:	www.countryfarmhouse.net
ROOMS:	2 Rooms; 1 Cottage; Private baths
CHILDREN:	Unable to accommodate
PETS:	Not allowed

Lavender Cookies

Makes 2 Dozen Cookies

$\frac{1}{4}$	**cup butter, softened**
$\frac{1}{2}$	**cup sugar**
1	**egg**
1	**tablespoon fresh lavender leaves, chopped (or 1 teaspoon dried) or 1 tablespoon fresh mint (1 teaspoon dried)**
1	**cup flour**
1	**teaspoon baking soda**
$\frac{1}{4}$	**teaspoon salt**

Preheat oven to 375°F. Cream butter and sugar. Stir in egg, and lavender or mint. Mix well.

In a separate bowl, sift flour, baking soda, and salt; add to creamed mixture. Drop by teaspoonfuls onto greased cookie sheet. Bake for 7-10 minutes.

The Filbert

"Life is grand at the Filbert"

The Filbert may well be the most supremely well-located bed and breakfast in northeast Pennsylvania. Located between the Lehigh Valley and the Pocono Mountains, it is a short distance from Philadelphia, Maryland, New York, and New Jersey. Yet, The Filbert is far removed from the chaos and clamor of the big cities. This well-restored ornate Victorian boasts a 60-foot-long porch complete with large, original fretwork. Many of the 200-year-old interior architectural details remain intact. The original wallpaper, dating to the late 1800s, continues to grace the walls.

The on-site general store, established in 1882, retains its original pressed-tin ceiling, wooden store counters, dry bins, and shelving. Pampering is also available on the premises: massage, skin, and nail care services may be reserved for your guaranteed relaxation.

INNKEEPERS:	Kathy and Terry Silfies
ADDRESS:	3740 Filbert Drive
	Danielsville, Pennsylvania 18038
TELEPHONE:	(610) 428-3300
E-MAIL:	filbertbnb@aol.com
WEBSITE:	www.filbertbnb.com
ROOMS:	4 Suites; 1 Family Suite; Private baths
CHILDREN:	Welcome
PETS:	Not allowed

Pumpkin Chip Cookies

Makes 3 Dozen Cookies

"These are the softest and best tasting chocolate chip cookies you will ever make." ~ Innkeeper, Filbert Bed & Breakfast

1	cup canned pumpkin
1	cup sugar
½	cup oil
1	egg, beaten
2	cups flour
2	teaspoons baking powder
1	teaspoon cinnamon
½	teaspoon salt
1	teaspoon milk mixed with 1 tablespoon baking soda
1	teaspoon vanilla
½	cup nuts (optional)
1	cup chocolate chips (can substitute butterscotch chips, if desired)

Preheat oven to 375°F. Mix pumpkin, sugar, oil, and beaten egg. Add remaining ingredients. Drop by teaspoonfuls on an ungreased cookie sheet.

Bake for 10-12 minutes.

Pineapple Hill

"In the 1700s, it was customary to place a pineapple on your front porch as a way of letting friends and neighbors know you were welcoming guests. We continue this tradition by offering the same hospitality to our guests. We hope you'll always feel welcome at Pineapple Hill." ~Innkeeper

The Pineapple Hill Bed and Breakfast Lodging rests between New Hope's center and Washington Crossing Park. Set on almost six acres, this Colonial manor house in Buck's County was built in 1790, and has 18-inch thick walls. On the grounds, the walls of the stone barn enclose a beautifully hand-tiled pool. The rose garden is situated where the springhouse once stood. The outdoor sitting area is surrounded by the ruins of the original summer kitchen.

"Your beautiful Pineapple Hill is a Bed & Breakfast dream!" ~ Guest

"Thanks for letting us share your little Eden." ~ Guest

INNKEEPERS:	Kathryn and Charles Triolo
ADDRESS:	1324 River Road
	New Hope, Pennsylvania 18938
TELEPHONE:	(215) 862-1790
E-MAIL:	innkeeper@pineapplehill.com
WEBSITE:	www.pineapplehill.com
ROOMS:	5 Rooms; 3 Suites; 1 Cottage; Private baths
CHILDREN:	Age 12 and older welcome
PETS:	Not allowed

Scottish Shortbread

Makes 2½ to 3 Dozen Cookies

1	pound butter, softened
1	cup sugar
1	teaspoon vanilla
4	cups flour

Additional ¼ cup sugar, for topping

Preheat oven to 300°F. Line a 9x13-inch baking pan with waxed paper. Combine and cream the first three ingredients. Add flour to the wet ingredients, 1 cup at a time. Spread dough in lined pan using a wet knife or metal spatula. Smooth to even out dough and prick all over with a fork. Bake for 40-60 minutes until pale golden color. Take out of oven and sprinkle with remaining ¼ cup sugar. Cut into serving-size pieces while still hot. Cool in pan.

Grandma's Ginger Snaps

Makes 4 Dozen Cookies

"My grandmother always baked these ginger snaps around the holidays.
They make the house smell wonderful!"
~ Innkeeper, Pineapple Hill Bed & Breakfast Lodging

2	**cups flour**
2	**teaspoons baking soda**
2	**teaspoons ginger**
½	**teaspoon cinnamon**
½	**teaspoon ground cloves**
¼	**teaspoon ground allspice**
6	**tablespoons butter**
⅓	**cup brown sugar**
¼	**cup honey**
¼	**cup dark molasses**

Preheat oven to 400°F. In a medium bowl, mix the first 6 ingredients; set aside.
In a heavy saucepan, mix the last 4 ingredients; melt over low heat and stir until
smooth and blended. Add flour mixture to butter/sugar mixture. Chill dough
in freezer for 5 minutes. Roll dough and cut with round cookie cutter. Place
cookies onto lightly greased cookie sheet. Bake for 13-15 minutes until slightly
cracked. Move from baking sheets to racks to cool.

Baba's Kolachke

Makes 4 to 6 Dozen Cookies

"Baba is Russian for Grandma, and this is a wonderful old recipe from the Russian side of the family." ~ Innkeeper, Pineapple Hill Bed & Breakfast Inn

4½	cups flour
3	teaspoons baking soda
1	pound butter
2	tablespoons sugar
4	eggs
½	pint sour cream

Lekvar Prune or Apricot Filling, or raspberry jam

Preheat oven to 350°F. In a medium bowl, mix the first 2 ingredients. In large bowl, cream the next 4 ingredients. Blend flour mixture into butter/sugar mixture. Knead dough until smooth. Roll dough and cut into 2x2-inch squares. Fold dough over filling to make triangles. Place cookies onto lightly greased cookie sheets. Bake for 13-15 minutes until slightly browned around edges. Move from baking sheets to racks to cool.

Three Gables Inn

Three Gables Inn is a Victorian Sears Catalogue house built in 1895 in Elgin, just seven miles from Corry. It is one of over 100,000 homes ordered from the Sears Roebuck Catalogue in the early 1900s and assembled by the owners. The fact that many of the homes are still in existence today attest to the quality and design of their construction.

At Three Gables Inn, the oak and chestnut woodwork complement the high ceilings. The dining room floor is unique with its alternating strips of cherry and maple wood. Treasures from the owner's travels to Thailand, China, Italy, and Australia are displayed throughout the home.

"We visited Lake Chautauqua, Lake Erie, a winery, Blair, the first oil well museum, and other sites in the area with helpful directions supplied by our hostess. The best part of our stay was the delightful Victorian decorated home of Peggy, who most graciously served a sumptuous, hearty breakfast each day." ~ Guest

INNKEEPERS:	Peggy Paul
ADDRESS:	18323 South Main Street
	Corry, Pennsylvania 16407
TELEPHONE:	(888) 640-5487
E-MAIL:	Not available
WEBSITE:	www.threegablesinn.net
ROOMS:	3 Rooms; Private baths
CHILDREN:	Welcome
PETS:	Not allowed

Fudge Sundae Pie

Makes 6 to 8 Servings

1	cup vanilla wafer crumbs
2	tablespoons sugar
2	tablespoons butter, melted
1	cup coconut, toasted
1	cup evaporated milk
1	cup semi-sweet chocolate bits
1	cup mini marshmallows
¼	teaspoon salt
1	quart vanilla ice cream
¾	cup pecan halves, for topping

Preheat oven to 350°F. Mix vanilla crumbs, sugar, melted butter, and toasted coconut. Press into an ungreased 9-inch pie pan.
Bake 5-6 minutes until set. Cool.

Place evaporated milk, chocolate bits, marshmallows, and salt in a double boiler; stir over heat until chocolate and marshmallows are melted. Cool.

Spoon half of the vanilla ice cream over the crust. Cover with half of the chocolate mixture. Repeat. Top with pecan halves. Freeze 3-5 hours.

Before serving, let pie sit at room temperature until softened.

Blue Ball

In spring and fall, watch the Amish farmers plant and harvest their crops from the Blue Ball Bed & Breakfast, located in the scenic Lancaster County countryside. Visit Amish woodworking, quilt, furniture, and craft shops. Dining with an Amish family may be arranged in advance. After a full day, unwind in the 6-person Jacuzzi in an enclosed patio attached to the inn. Thoughtful details abound at the Blue Ball Bed & Breakfast: soft terry robes and slippers, and delightfully thick towels.

The inn is minutes away from Sight and Sound American Music Theatre, museums, antique stores, and factory outlet shopping. Blue Ball B&B is just a short distance from the towns of Intercourse, Bird-in-Hand, and Paradise. Quilting weekends are available.

INNKEEPERS:	Frank and Jeanne Warsheski
ADDRESS:	1075 Main Street
	Blue Ball, Pennsylvania 17506
TELEPHONE:	(717) 355-9994; (800) 720-9827
E-MAIL:	pudone@ptd.net
WEBSITE:	www.blueballbandb.com
ROOMS:	4 Rooms; 2 Suites; Private baths
CHILDREN:	Welcome
PETS:	Small pets allowed; Resident cat

Jeanne's Pumpkin Bars

Makes 12 Bars

"These are a healthy, smart, low-fat treat."
~ Innkeeper, Blue Ball Bed & Breakfast

1 **(16-ounce) can pumpkin**
1 **box spice cake mix**
Cool Whip, for topping (optional)

Preheat oven to 350°F. Combine pumpkin and the spice cake mix. Stir the stiff batter well until all of the cake mix is moistened. Spread batter in a 9x12-inch cake pan and bake according to the cake mix box directions. Cool. Serve with Cool Whip, if desired.

Apple Bin Inn

APPLE BIN INN
🍎 Bed & Breakfast 🍎

At the Apple Bin Inn, the proximity of the Amish neighbors provides a daily reminder to slow down and focus on the simpler things in life.

As you turn into the driveway, you'll be welcomed by an acre of park-like tranquility. Enter the main house as friends do, through the back door, and into the kitchen with an arched-brick hearth. The country dining room has the original wide-plank flooring and is the staging area for the scrumptious breakfast that will await you each morning. The comfortable living room features an extensive library to suit all reading tastes, along with comfy sofas and chairs for reading, knitting, games, or just talking with newfound friends. Once settled into a beautiful guest room, suite, or cottage, you'll know that the Apple Bin Inn combines the best of both worlds. Snuggle up under an antique family heirloom quilt and check the e-mail messages on your laptop computer using the inn's free wireless Internet access. During the summer months, the in-ground swimming pool will beckon you to take time to refresh and re-energize.

INNKEEPERS:	Steve and Jamie Shane
ADDRESS:	2835 Willow Street Pike
	Willow Street, Pennsylvania (Lancaster County) 17584
TELEPHONE:	(717) 464-5881; (800) 338-4296
E-MAIL:	stay@applebininn.com
WEBSITE:	www.applebininn.com
ROOMS:	5 Rooms; 2 Suites; 1 Cottage; Private baths
CHILDREN:	Welcome
PETS:	Not allowed; Resident cats

Chess Squares

Makes 8 to 12 Servings

*"This recipe was a favorite of friends and neighbors when we lived
in Nashville. Now, our Lancaster County guests love them too!"*
~ Innkeeper, Apple Bin Inn Bed & Breakfast

Layer 1:
1	box yellow butter cake mix
1	stick unsalted butter, melted
1	egg, beaten

Layer 2:
3	eggs, beaten
1	(16-ounce) box powdered sugar
1	(8-ounce) package cream cheese
1	teaspoon vanilla extract

Dash of salt

Preheat oven to 300°F. Mix the layer 1 ingredients, and pack on bottom and
sides of a greased 11x14-inch pan. Cream the layer 2 ingredients, and spread on
top of layer 1 ingredients. Bake for 60-65 minutes. Cool, then turn out of pan
and cut into brownie-size pieces (a plastic knife works best).

Mill Creek Homestead

The Mill Creek Homestead stands along a two-lane country road in the village of Bird-in-Hand. The 1793 stone house is accented by towering pine trees that limit a distant view, but you may see Amish neighbors working in their tobacco or cornfields or hanging tobacco in the barn to dry. Guests in the otherwise enveloping silence will probably notice the sound of horse and buggies passing by.

Many visitors inquire about the origination of the village name, Bird-in-Hand. At the time that Old Philadelphia Pike was being laid out between Lancaster and Philadelphia, road surveyors were making McNabb's Hotel their headquarters. The sign in front of the inn portrayed a man with a bird in his hand, and the hotel soon became known as the Bird-in-Hand Inn. This hotel designation became the landmark identifying the area. Variations of the original sign appear throughout the town today.

INNKEEPERS:	Vicki and Frank Alfone
ADDRESS:	2578 Old Philadelphia Pike
	Bird-in-Hand (Lancaster County) Pennsylvania 17505
TELEPHONE:	(717) 291-6419; (8000 771-2578
E-MAIL:	millcreekbnb@hotmail.com
WEBSITE:	www.millcreekhomestead.com
ROOMS:	4 Rooms; Private baths
CHILDREN:	Age 10 and older welcome
PETS:	Not allowed

Apricot Pecan Bars

Makes 32 Bars

"These are easy and tasty fruit-and-nut bars."
~ Innkeeper, Mill Creek Homestead Bed & Breakfast

1½	cups flour
⅔	cup sugar
½	teaspoon cinnamon
1½	sticks margarine
2	egg yolks
1	teaspoon vanilla
½	cup apricot preserves
¾	cup pecans, chopped

Preheat oven to 425°F. Mix the flour, sugar, and cinnamon. Cut in margarine until mixture resembles coarse meal. Add egg yolks and vanilla. Press ¾ of the dough evenly into the bottom of a greased 9-inch square pan. Spread preserves over dough. Crumble remaining dough over preserves and sprinkle with nuts. Bake for 20-25 minutes.

Lemon Olive Oil Cake

Makes 8 Servings

"This is an incredibly light and airy cake."
~ Innkeeper, Mill Creek Homestead Bed & Breakfast

5	eggs, separated
¾	cup plus 1½ teaspoons sugar, divided
¾	cup olive oil
1½	tablespoons lemon juice
1	cup flour
1½	teaspoons lemon zest

Preheat oven to 350°F. In a medium bowl, beat egg yolks and ½ cup sugar. Add olive oil and lemon juice. Add flour and lemon zest; mix just until combined.

In a separate bowl, beat egg whites until foamy. Continue to beat the whites, while gradually adding ¼ cup sugar; beat until soft peaks form. Gently and gradually fold egg white mixture into egg yolk mixture. Pour batter into a greased and parchment-lined springform pan while tapping gently on the outside of the pan.

Sprinkle 1½ teaspoons sugar on top of the batter. Bake for 45 minutes. Cool for 10 minutes before removing the springform pan.

Applesauce Gingerbread with Pears

Makes 8 Servings

"...Great variation of an old favorite." ~ Innkeeper, Mill Creek Bed & Breakfast

1	**(8-ounce) can pear halves**
6	**tablespoons oil**
1/3	**cup sugar**
1	**egg**
1/2	**cup molasses**
1/3	**cup applesauce**
1/3	**cup sour cream**
1¾	**cups flour**
1	**teaspoon baking soda**
1	**teaspoon cinnamon**
1/2	**teaspoon ginger**
1/8	**cup powdered sugar, for garnish**

Preheat oven to 350°F. Drain pears; place in bottom of greased 9x12-inch baking dish. Mix oil, sugar, egg, molasses, applesauce, and sour cream. Add all dry ingredients; mix. Pour over pears and bake for 30 minutes. Let cool for 10 minutes. Cut into squares and serve with powdered sugar sprinkled on top.

The Inn at Starlight Lake

"Sit back, watch the world go by, and remember;
everything is better by Starlight."

The history of The Inn at Starlight Lake began in 1806 when a Connecticut settler named Underwood acquired 10,000 acres of rolling hills in northeastern Pennsylvania. In 1880, his grandson built a dam at the outlet of a small pond, and expanding it into a large body of water he named "Starlight Lake." Eugene Fay bought a tract of land near the eastern shore of the lake in 1907 and built a summer boarding house he called "Starlight Inn."

Today, The Inn at Starlight Lake is very family-friendly, and accommodates visitors in the Main House and three cottages. A plethora of activities, inside, around the inn, and on the lake are available to fulfill the recreation and entertainment needs of guests young, old, and in-between. Breakfast, lunch, and dinner may be enjoyed in the informal lakeside dining room. All pastas and desserts, including ice creams, are made on the premises.

INNKEEPERS: Sari and Jimmy Schwartz
ADDRESS: 289 Starlight Lake Road
Starlight, Pennsylvania 18461
TELEPHONE: (570) 798-2519; (800) 248-2519
E-MAIL: info@innatstarlightlake.com
WEBSITE: www.innatstarlightlake.com
ROOMS: 22 Rooms; 1 Suite; Private & shared baths
CHILDREN: Welcome
PETS: Welcome

Sour Cream Apple Pie

Makes 8 Servings

"This recipe was awarded the Delaware Highlands Conservatory Best Pie."
~ Innkeeper, Inn at Starlight Lake

1	(10-inch) deep pie shell

For the filling:

¼	cup flour
1	cup sugar
2	eggs, beaten
2	cups sour cream
1	teaspoon vanilla extract
1	teaspoon nutmeg
6	medium apples, peeled and coarsely grated

For the topping:

⅓	cup brown sugar, packed
⅔	cup flour
2	teaspoons cinnamon
½	stick butter, softened

For the filling: Preheat oven to 400°F. Mix the filling ingredients and pour into pie shell. Bake for 15 minutes, then lower oven temperature to 350°F, and bake for 30-45 minutes more, or until set.

For the topping: Mix topping ingredients. When pie is baked, remove from the oven and set oven temperature to 400°F. Sprinkle topping over pie and return the pie to the oven for 5-10 minutes, or until topping is browned.

The Inn on Maple Street

"The Family and Pet Friendly Bed & Breakfast"

One block from historic Route 6, in the mountains of northwest Pennsylvania's McKean County, you'll find the Inn on Maple Street. Cookies come fresh from the oven at this bed and breakfast, and fireflies dance on the lawn at night. Make your entrance through the unusual banker's door that has a stained-glass side panel in the prairie design of Frank Lloyd Wright. You'll see the stately old upright piano to appease guest's lyrical moods, and an impressive oak staircase. A classic chess set is ready for a match of wits in the Library Room. Shelves of paperbacks are for the taking, with a "take one, leave one" philosophy. The focus of the Parlor Room is on electronic entertainment and big bowls of popcorn. In each guestroom, you'll find tall windows with shutters and lace curtains, and a hand-crocheted afghan on every bed.

"...Outstanding Breakfast," is one guest's reaction to the breakfast buffet by candlelight in the Breakfast Room.

INNKEEPERS:	Jay D. Roush
ADDRESS:	115 Maple Street (one block off Route 6)
	Port Allegany, Pennsylvania 16743
TELEPHONE:	(814) 642-5171
E-MAIL:	innonmaplest@pennswoods.net
WEBSITE:	www.theinnonmaplestreet.com
ROOMS:	4 Rooms; 1 Suite; Private & shared baths
CHILDREN:	Welcome
PETS:	Welcome; Resident dog

Seven Spice Cake

Makes 8 Servings

"Guests can never guess the seven spices used in this moist cake."
~ Innkeeper, Inn on Maple Street Bed & Breakfast

2½	cups flour
¼	teaspoon baking powder
1½	teaspoons baking soda
1	teaspoon cinnamon
½	teaspoon ground cloves
½	teaspoon ground allspice
½	teaspoon ground ginger
½	teaspoon ground mace
½	teaspoon ground white pepper
¼	teaspoon ground cardamom
1	cup butter or margarine
1	cup sugar
1	egg
½	cup apple juice
2	cups applesauce
½	cup walnuts, finely chopped (optional)

Powdered sugar, for garnish
Whipped cream, for garnish

Preheat oven to 350°F. Grease and flour a bundt pan or 9x13-inch baking pan. In a medium bowl, sift the flour, baking powder, baking soda, cinnamon, cloves, allspice, ginger, mace, white pepper, and cardamom; set aside.

In a large bowl, beat the butter and sugar until fluffy. Add egg and apple juice; mix well. Add flour mixture alternately with applesauce to butter mixture, mixing well after each addition. Stir in walnuts, if desired. Pour batter into pan and bake for 45-50 minutes. Cool cake. Sift powdered sugar over top of cake and garnish with a dollop of whipped cream.

Tara – A Country Inn

Inspired by the movie, *Gone With the Wind*, Tara – A Country Inn, offers you a lasting impression of southern hospitality. Innkeepers Donna and Jim Winner are passionate *Gone With the Wind* historians. One of their prized acquisitions displayed at the inn is the robe worn by actress Vivian Leigh during the honeymoon scene in the movie.

This 1854 mansion has twenty-seven luxurious guestrooms with fireplaces and Jacuzzis. A view of the 450-acre Shenango Lake; Frederick Remington bronze statuary within Tara's impressive formal gardens; a heated swimming pool; complimentary bicycles; and gourmet and casual dining are just a few of the special amenities. Tara is a virtual museum of Civil War and *Gone With the Wind* memorabilia. Tours with the knowledgeable inn guides are encouraged. As a setting for romantic getaways, weddings, meetings, or private parties, it is ideal.

INNKEEPERS:	Donna and Jim Winner
ADDRESS:	2844 Lake Road
	Clark, Pennsylvania 16113
TELEPHONE:	(724) 962-3535; (800) 782-2803
E-MAIL:	info@tara-inn.com
WEBSITE:	www.tara-inn.com
ROOMS:	24 Rooms; 3 Suites; Private baths
CHILDREN:	Age 12 and older welcome
PETS:	Not allowed

The Swans of Tara

Makes 6 Servings

"...A signature dish at Tara – A Country Inn since 1986."
~ Innkeeper, Tara – A Country Inn

Pastry Swans:
½   **cup milk**
1½   **tablespoons butter**
Pinch salt
½   **cup plus 2 tablespoons bread flour**
3   **eggs**

Mousse:
¾   **cup sugar**
4   **eggs**
3   **egg yolks**
2   **tablespoons unflavored gelatin**
⅓   **cup Grand Marnier**
1½   **cups whipping cream**
1   **teaspoon vanilla**
Powdered sugar, to taste

Pastry Swans:
Preheat oven to 400°F. In a 1 quart saucepan, combine milk, butter, and salt; bring to a full boil. Remove from heat. Gradually mix in flour until pastry is smooth and rolls free from sides of pan. Beat in eggs, one at a time, until medium-stiff consistency. Shape into 6 "S" shaped necks and 6, 2-inch ovals for bodies. The body ovals need to have a slight bowl shape to allow for filling. Place on a greased baking sheet and bake 15-20 minutes.

Mousse:
In large bowl and using an electric mixer, beat sugar, eggs, and yolks at high speed until eggs form a thick ribbon, about 12 minutes. In the top of a small double boiler over simmering water, dissolve gelatin in Grand Marnier. Pour into egg mixture. Whip cream with vanilla and fold into mixture. Spoon into 6 pastry swan bodies, insert necks, and top with sugar. Refrigerate for 2 hours.

Greystone Manor

The quiet charm of the Greystone Manor is evident as soon as you enter the Victorian lobby. Leaded, beveled glass doors, and plaster-cast wall and ceiling sculptures add to the warm and cozy feeling of the inn. Set on top of a hill on two acres, this brick mansion is in the heart of Amish Country. The Greystone Manor was constructed in 1883 from a farmhouse built in the mid-1800s. Originally a barn, the Carriage House is guest-ready with pleasing country decor. Amenities include numerous patios, outdoor pool and hot tub, gardens, and ponds. Consider taking a buggy ride, visiting an Amish homestead, attending a performance at the Amish Experience Theatre, or touring the Americana Museum while staying in the village of Bird-In-Hand.

INNKEEPERS:	Angela and Wade Skiadas
ADDRESS:	2658 Old Philadelphia Pike
	Bird-in-Hand, Pennsylvania 17505
TELEPHONE:	(717) 393-4233
E-MAIL:	angela@greystonemanor.com
WEBSITE:	www.greystonemanor.com
ROOMS:	6 Rooms; 4 Suites; Private baths
CHILDREN:	Welcome
PETS:	Welcome; Resident dog

Pennsylvania Dutch Bread Pudding

Makes 8 Servings

"This pudding is great for breakfast or as a dessert."
~ Innkeeper, Greystone Manor Bed & Breakfast

4	cups bread, cubed
½	cup raisins
2	cups milk
½	cup butter
½	teaspoon nutmeg
½	cup sugar
1	teaspoon vanilla
½	teaspoon cinnamon

Preheat oven to 350°F. Combine bread and raisins in a 1-quart saucepan; add milk and ½ cup butter. Cook over medium heat until butter is melted; pour over bread mixture. Stir in remaining ingredients. Pour into a greased 1½ quart casserole dish. Bake for 40-50 minutes until center is set.

Harvest Moon

The Harvest Moon Bed and Breakfast is a turn-of-the-century guesthouse in a timeless part of the world where values and a sense of culture run deep. New Holland is a place where church bells still toll, and home-baked goods are prevalent in the area restaurants. Furniture makers, quilters crafting in differing styles, and the renowned New Holland Horse Stables are yours to discover during your sojourn.

Your hosts at the Harvest Moon are chefs. Emphasis is placed on the craft, history, and understanding of fine dining at their inn. Italian, Holiday, German, Holistic, and the ever-popular Chocolate Weekends are culinary events at the Harvest Moon. Wine and cheese tours are also on their schedule of momentous occasions. Sample the area's finest wines and visit Amish-run dairy farms with real cheese caves.

INNKEEPERS:	Carl and Marlies Kosko
ADDRESS:	311 E. Main St.
	New Holland, Pennsylvania 17557
TELEPHONE:	(717) 354-0213; (888) 824-3763
E-MAIL:	info@harvestmoonbandb.com
WEBSITE:	www.harvestmoonbandb.com
ROOMS:	4 Rooms; 4 Private baths
CHILDREN:	Welcome
PETS:	Not allowed

Strawberry Rhubarb Strudel

Makes 8 Servings

"This is a great recipe for the springtime, just when the strawberries are coming out and the rhubarb is ending. If your season runs differently, try freezing some rhubarb for this special recipe."
~ Innkeeper, Harvest Moon Bed & Breakfast

$\frac{1}{2}$ **stick butter**
$\frac{1}{2}$ **package phyllo dough (recipe calls for 1 sleeve; package contains 2 sleeves)**

Filling:
3   **cups strawberries, cleaned, cut in half**
2   **cups rhubarb, cleaned, and cut in 1-inch cubes**
$\frac{1}{2}$ **cup sugar or a bit more, to taste**
$\frac{1}{8}$ **cup of flour**
$\frac{1}{2}$ **teaspoon of cinnamon**
$\frac{1}{4}$ **teaspoon ginger**
Pinch of cloves
Pinch of salt
Juice from $\frac{1}{2}$ lemon
Vanilla sauce or ice cream, for topping

Preheat oven to 350°F. Melt $\frac{1}{2}$-stick of butter and set aside. Remove one sheet of phyllo dough and unroll. Place the sheet of dough in a rimmed cookie sheet. Brush dough with butter. Place a second sheet off to the side of the first to extend the length of the strudel to the full size of the pan; brush with butter. Continue this process until all of the sheets of phyllo have been buttered and placed in the pan.

For the filling: In a bowl, mix all filling ingredients in the order in which they are listed. Top phyllo sheets with the strawberry mixture. Roll the phyllo up around the filling and be sure that it is tightly wrapped. Brush the top of the roll with butter and sprinkle with sugar. Bake for about 40 minutes until top of roll is golden brown and a bit of the liquid bubbles out of the side. Let cool. Enjoy with your favorite vanilla sauce or ice cream.

The McMurray House

Like the generations before them, Harry and Rosemary McMurray are carrying on the family tradition as innkeepers on sixty-five acres of family-owned property. Slippery Rock is the town where the McMurray House, with its horses and white fences, create their peaceful scene. The Old Stone House, an historical landmark built in 1822, is one mile from the bed and breakfast. This is where the McMurray forebears lived and served meals to travelers.

The settlement of Slippery Rock was known to its original residents as Ginger Hill, a name that legends say arose from a local tavernkeeper's practice of giving plenty of ginger with the whiskey he sold. In 1824, the first post office for the newly settled area was built on the banks of Slippery Rock Creek. The post office was moved to its present location in 1826. In 1900, the name of the community was changed to Slippery Rock to correspond with the name of the post office.

INNKEEPERS:	Harry and Rosemary McMurray
ADDRESS:	258 Centreville Pike
	Slippery Rock, Pennsylvania 16057
TELEPHONE:	(724) 794 8188
E-MAIL:	mcmurrayhouse@zoominternet.net
WEBSITE:	www.mcmurrayhouse.com
ROOMS:	1 Suite; Private bath
CHILDREN:	Age 13 and older welcome
PETS:	Not allowed

Sugar Plums

Makes 8 Servings

"This is a wonderful holiday treat, but good year 'round as well."
~ Innkeeper, McMurray House Bed & Breakfast

2	eggs, beaten
1½	cup sugar, divided
1	cup dried dates, pitted and chopped
1	cup coconut
1	cup walnuts, chopped
1	teaspoon vanilla extract

Preheat oven to 375°F. Blend eggs and 1 cup of sugar. Stir in dates, coconut, walnuts, and vanilla. Butter a 2-quart casserole dish. Pour mixture into the dish. Bake for 30 minutes, stirring every 10 minutes. Remove from the oven and let cool until mixture can be handled. Roll into walnut size balls. Roll balls in remaining sugar.

Meringue Topped Rhubarb Dessert

Makes 9 to 12 servings

"It is easy to grow rhubarb in Pennsylvania. Serving a rhubarb dessert
at the McMurray House makes it easy to please our guests."
~ Innkeeper, McMurray House Bed & Breakfast

Crust:

1	cup flour
2	tablespoons sugar
½	cup butter or margarine

Filling:

4	cups rhubarb, chopped
1½	cups sugar
¼	cup flour
1	tablespoon orange zest, grated
⅓	cup milk
3	egg yolks, beaten

Meringue:

3	egg whites
⅛	teaspoon salt
6	tablespoons sugar

For the crust: Preheat oven to 325°F. Combine flour and sugar. Cut in butter with a pastry blender until the mixture looks like coarse meal. Pat into an ungreased 9-inch square pan. Bake for 20 minutes until lightly brown. Cool 5 minutes.

For the filling: Combine rhubarb, sugar, flour, and orange zest; mix well. Add milk and eggs yolks; stir well. Pour rhubarb mixture into the baked crust. Bake for 45 minutes at 325°F.

For the meringue: Preheat oven to 400°F. In a small bowl, combine egg whites and salt; beat until soft peaks form. Spread meringue on the baked rhubarb. Bake for 8-10 minutes until the meringue is lightly browned. Cool on rack.

Pineapple Raspberry Torte

Makes 12 Servings

"Special occasions call for Pineapple Raspberry Torte at the McMurray House Bed & Breakfast." ~ Innkeeper, McMurray House Bed & Breakfast

1	(4-serving size) Jell-O-Brand Raspberry Flavor Gelatin
1¼	cups boiling water
1	(20-ounce) can crushed pineapple (Do not drain.)
2	(9-inch) white cake layers, baked and cooled
1¾	cups Cool Whip

Dissolve gelatin in boiling water. Stir in undrained pineapple; chill until very thick. Spread ½ of the gelatin mixture on top of each cake layer and chill until firm, about 3 hours. Spread ½ of the whipped topping over each gelatin layer. Place the second cake layer on top of the first, gelatin-side up. Chill.

Keystone Inn

Keystone Inn is in a residential area of Gettysburg, away from the commercialism and busyness of downtown, but only five blocks from Lincoln Square. Built by a local furniture maker in 1913, the quality craftsmanship is evident in this late Victorian-style brick home. A wide-columned porch hugs the north and west sides of the house. Inside the huge leaded-glass main entrance, you'll see the chestnut staircase marching majestically to the third floor. Copious amounts of natural oak and chestnut are found throughout the house. Chestnut was used almost exclusively in the first floor rooms, and oak is found in abundance in the rest of the house. The quiet guestrooms stand behind massive, two-inch thick doors.

"We slept like lambs." ~ Guest

"This place is cleaner than my mother-in-laws place, and she's the 'Queen of Clean.' "~ Guest

INNKEEPERS:	Doris and Wilmer Martin
ADDRESS:	231 Hanover Street
	Gettysburg, Pennsylvania 17325
TELEPHONE:	(717) 337-3888
E-MAIL:	keystoneinnbb@yahoo.com
WEBSITE:	www.keystoneinnbb.com
ROOMS:	4 Rooms; 1 Suite; Private baths
CHILDREN:	Welcome
PETS:	Not allowed

Any Fruit Shortcake

Makes 10 to 12 Servings

did V! not like

Cake:

2	cups flour
1	cup sugar
2½	teaspoons baking powder
⅓	cup vegetable oil
⅔	cup milk
1	egg
1	teaspoon vanilla

Preheat oven to 350°F. Combine dry ingredients. Add the wet ingredients. Beat 50 strokes. Pour into a greased 9x9-inch baking dish and bake for about 35 minutes.

Basic Topping:

1	cup sugar
2	tablespoons cornstarch
1	cup water

Combine sugar and cornstarch in a small saucepan. Add water. Bring to a boil. Remove from the stove.

The following variations may be added to the basic topping recipe:

Strawberry - Add a few drops of red food coloring to the sauce. Cool. Add 1 quart of diced strawberries. Top each slice of cake with ½ cup of strawberry mixture and whipped cream, if desired.

Peach – 2 fresh peaches, peeled and sliced. Add ½ teaspoon cinnamon to the sauce. Cool. Add peaches. Top slices of cake with ½ cup of peach mixture and top with whipped cream, if desired.

Apple –2 peeled and diced apples. Add ½ teaspoon cinnamon to sauce. Cool. Add apples. Top slices of cake with ½ cup of apple mixture and top with whipped cream, if desired.

Blueberry -1 quart blueberries. Add a few drops of blue food coloring to sauce. Cool. Add blueberries. Top slices of cake with ½ cup of blueberry mixture and top with whipped cream, if desired.

Rocky Springs

O n seventeen acres along the Conestoga River, called Rocky Springs Park, sits a restored mansion house dating back to the mid-1800s. Extravagant five-course breakfasts are served to the travelers who have chosen to be overnight guests in this pre-Victorian home, now known as Rocky Springs Bed and Breakfast. Each guest room has a commanding view of the park, formerly an amusement park that was in its heyday during the early 1900s. The deck adjacent to the dining room is made of wood from the old roller coaster.

Lancaster County Central Park is within walking distance from Rocky Springs. Here are just a few of the features to explore in this park's 544 acres: a public swimming pool; skate park; innumerable trails for hiking, biking, and cross-country skiing; Historic Rockford Plantation; a Revolutionary War–era house museum; an environmental library; The Garden of Five Senses. Tree-to-tasting maple sugar events are held each spring.

INNKEEPERS:	Glori and Nevin Brubaker
ADDRESS:	1441 Millport Road
	Lancaster, Pennsylvania 17602
TELEPHONE:	(717) 509-6800; (866) 611-4647
E-MAIL:	innkeeper@rockyspringsbnb.com
WEBSITE:	www.rockyspringsbnb.com
ROOMS:	4 Rooms; 1 Cottage; Private baths
CHILDREN:	Age 12 and older welcome
PETS:	Not allowed; Resident cat

Decadent Pumpkin Torte

Makes 8 to 10 Servings

"Enjoy the juxtaposition of sweet and sour, chocolate and pumpkin, coffee and cream. ...An unexpected bliss. Plan ahead, this dessert needs to be prepared several hours before serving." ~ Chef, Rocky Springs Bed & Breakfast

4	cups whole milk vanilla yogurt
1	cup cinnamon graham crackers, crushed
1	cup chocolate graham crackers, crushed
3	tablespoons plus 1 cup brown sugar, firmly packed
3	tablespoons butter, melted
2	eggs
2	cups freshly cooked pumpkin, puréed
2	teaspoons vanilla extract
$\frac{1}{2}$	teaspoon salt
$\frac{1}{2}$	teaspoon cinnamon, plus extra for garnish
$\frac{1}{2}$	teaspoon allspice
$\frac{1}{4}$	teaspoon nutmeg

Irish cream syrup for topping
Fresh whipped cream, for topping
Chocolate shavings, for garnish

Preheat oven to 325°F. Put yogurt in a large sieve lined with a coffee filter. Place the sieve over a bowl and drain for 8 hours in the refrigerator.

Combine cinnamon and chocolate graham cracker crumbs, 3 tablespoons of brown sugar, and butter; press into a 9-inch springform pan.
In a medium bowl, combine drained yogurt solids, eggs, pumpkin, 1 cup of brown sugar, vanilla, salt, $\frac{1}{2}$ teaspoon of cinnamon, allspice, and nutmeg; pour into crust. Bake for 60 minutes, or until set. Chill for several hours.
To serve, drizzle each serving generously with Irish cream syrup, dollup with whipped cream, and sprinkle with cinnamon and chocolate shavings.

Hamanassett

T he historic registry mansion of Hamanassett in the Brandywine Valley continues a centuries-old tradition of hospitality, one guest at a time. Past and present converge the moment you enter the Grand Hall.

"...located on the top and slope of a fine hill with more than three-fourths of the land covered with a luxuriant growth of noble woods...it was modeled on Downings Northern Farmhouse built of hard, dark gray stone taken from the land...and he chose the Indian name of a small river by which his forefathers had settled [in 1647], and he called it 'HAMANASSETT'."
From the Memoir of Dr. Charles D. Meigs (1792-1869)
The description is still accurate today.

"...A perfect retreat away from the world and into a secret garden." ~ Guest

"The elaborate breakfasts are a high point." ~ New York Times

INNKEEPERS:	Ashley Mon
ADDRESS:	115 Indian Springs Drive
	Chester Heights, Pennsylvania 19017
TELEPHONE:	(610) 459-3000; (877) 836-8212
E-MAIL:	stay@hamanassett.com
WEBSITE:	www.hamanassett.com
ROOMS:	5 Rooms; 2 Suites; and Carriage House; all private baths
CHILDREN:	Age 12 and older welcome; Under age 12 allowed in Carriage House
PETS:	Welcome in the Carriage House; Resident pet

Blueberry Brûlée

Makes 6 Servings

"We serve this hot in the winter. In the summer, we make it the day before and serve it chilled. Either way, it is delicious and healthy."
~ Innkeeper, Hamanassett Bed & Breakfast

1½	**cups granola**
3	**cups blueberries**
1	**cup vanilla yogurt**
1	**cup brown sugar**

Place ¼ cup of granola in the bottom of a 1 cup size ramekin measuring 3½ inches in diameter. Add ½ cup of blueberries on top of the granola. Spread a thin layer of yogurt over the top of the blueberries. Sprinkle brown sugar over the yogurt. Broil on top rack of oven 3-5 minutes until the brown sugar is caramelized. It can be kept in a warm oven for up to 30 minutes.

If serving cold, remove from the oven and let cool. Refrigerate.

Failte Inn

Failte (pronounced Fall-Cha) is the Gaelic word for welcome.

Failte Inn is in the Susquehanna River Valley amid the Endless Mountains of rural Pennsylvania. The site of the inn overlooks acres of green lawns, apple orchards, flower gardens, and fountains. Feel the cool mountain breezes during the lazy days of summer, or warm up in front of a fireplace in the parlor or well-stocked library on a cool winter's day. Listen to the quiet, or compose your own fine music on the antique baby grand piano.

The Failte Inn offers complimentary carafes of Mead (honeyed wine) from days of old in their private pub, which was operated as a speakeasy during the days of Prohibition. There is an outdoor spa where you can soak as you stargaze. The on-site antique shop specializes in finer Victoriana.

INNKEEPERS:	Jim, Sarah, and Jamie True
ADDRESS:	RR# 2 Box 323 Sheshequin
	Athens, Pennsylvania 18810
TELEPHONE:	(570) 358-3899
E-MAIL:	thefailteinn@webtv.net
WEBSITE:	www.failteinn.com
ROOMS:	5 Rooms; 2 Suites; Private baths
CHILDREN:	Welcome
PETS:	Not allowed; Resident cat

Tortilla Dessert

Makes 10 Servings

"This is a delicious and easy breakfast treat. You may use any kind of preserves or use 1/4 cup of chocolate chips instead of preserves."
~ Innkeeper, Failte Inn Bed & Breakfast

1	(10-count) package (6-8inch rounds) flour tortillas
1	(8-ounce) package cream cheese, softened
1	(16-ounce) jar cherry preserves
10	tablespoons butter or margarine
$\frac{1}{2}$	cup sugar
1	teaspoon cinnamon

Powdered sugar, for garnish

Preheat oven to 350°F. Spread butter on one side of tortilla. Turn over. Lightly spread the other side with both cream cheese and cherry preserves. Roll up with the cream cheese and preserves to the inside. Sprinkle with a mixture of sugar and cinnamon. Place in a greased pan and bake for 15-20 minutes. Sprinkle with powdered sugar and serve warm.

Bed and Breakfast at Natural Acres

S ituated amidst a 550-acre fully operating Certified Organic Farm, Bed and Breakfast at Natural Acres is a simple, brick farmhouse in Central Pennsylvania's Dauphin County. The organic lifestyle is an essential part of the accommodations. Start your day with a wake-up call from the farm's rooster, and breakfast made from the healthiest farm-fresh, organic eggs and produce.

Take a ride in the inn's horse-drawn carriage, or ride a bike on the farm lanes across the rolling produce fields. You can tour the farm, feed the free-range chickens, and learn more about the ecologically sound farming practices. Just a stone's throw away from the bed and breakfast is Natural Acres Market. A variety of organic meats, produce, supplements, and a broad range of educational books are sold.

Stop by the bakery and see what's hot out of the oven.

INNKEEPERS:	Cheryl Nolt
ADDRESS:	175 Maple Drive
	Millersburg, Pennsylvania 17061
TELEPHONE:	(717) 692-1000
E-MAIL:	naturalacres@epix.net
WEBSITE:	www.naturalacresbedandbreakfast.com
ROOMS:	5 Rooms; 5 Private baths
CHILDREN:	Age 12 and older welcome
PETS:	Not allowed

Apple Crisp

Makes 6 Servings

"Served warm with vanilla ice cream, this dessert can't be beat."
~ Innkeeper, Bed and Breakfast at Natural Acres

4	cups apples, sliced
⅔ - ¾	cup brown sugar, packed
½	cup flour
½	cup quick oats
¾	teaspoon nutmeg
1	teaspoon cinnamon
⅓	cup butter, softened

Preheat oven to 350°F. Put apples in an 8x8-inch baking dish. In a bowl, combine the remaining ingredients. Spoon the mixture on top of the apples. Bake for 25 minutes until apples are soft.

Sheppard Mansion

The "House That Shoes Built" in 1913 is now the Sheppard Mansion Bed and Breakfast, located in downtown Hanover. The family of H.A. Sheppard, Hanover Shoes co-founder, inhabited the home until Mrs. Sheppard's death in 1960. Maintained, but unoccupied by family members until 1998, Mr. and Mrs. Sheppard's descendants decided to restore the mansion to its original state and give the building a second life as a bed and breakfast.

Cloud-like beds and crisp linens epitomize the opulence in the nine Sheppard Mansion guest rooms. The early 1800 Fisher's Guest Cottage is the newest addition to the accommodations, lodging up to four guests.

Executive Chef Andrew Little brings his vision of "farm to table" to the dining room on Wednesday through Saturday evenings. By using the finest local produce, and using homebred cattle as part of the ever-changing and innovative menu, Chef Little is able to oversee all aspects of his feasts for your palate.

INNKEEPERS:	Timothy Bob
ADDRESS:	117 Frederick Street
	Hanover, Pennsylvania 17331
TELEPHONE:	(717) 633-8075; (877) S-MANSION
E-MAIL:	reservations@sheppardmansion.com
WEBSITE:	www.sheppardmansion.com
ROOMS:	9 Rooms; 1 Cottage; Private baths
CHILDREN:	Age 12 and older welcome
PETS:	Welcome in the Cottage with deposit

Campari and Lemon Verbena Sorbet

"This is one of my favorite sorbet flavors. Many times, sorbets are VERY sweet and end up masking the true flavor which is the star of the show. This particular sorbet is perfect for a hot summer night, as the bitterness of the grapefruit and the herbal notes of the verbena balance the sugar required for a sorbet. The egg whites add a luxurious texture and, as always, use very fresh eggs, and omit if serving to the elderly or children." ~ Chef, Sheppard Mansion

$1\frac{1}{4}$	**cups sugar**
1	**cup water**
$2\frac{1}{2}$	**cups grapefruit juice**
$\frac{1}{4}$	**cup Campari**
1	**ounce lemon verbena**
1	**ounce fresh cracked black pepper**
2	**egg whites**
10	**ounces Perrier bottled water**

Combine the sugar, water, grapefruit juice, Campari, verbena, and cracked pepper in a non-reactive sauce pot. Bring the mixture to a boil and remove from heat. Cover the pot and let infuse for 30 minutes. Strain the liquid through a fine mesh strainer and chill in the refrigerator overnight. The next day, foam the egg whites and add to the Perrier.

Combine this mixture with the grapefruit mix. Process this mix in an ice cream maker based on the individual manufacturer's specifications.

House at the End of the Road

The House at the End of the Road is a pre-1900 farmhouse tucked away from time and traffic on twenty-five wooded acres in the western Pennsylvania town of Summerville. The Inn's Willow Bedroom looks out on the 100-year-old willow tree and the original post-and-beam barn. Bring your fly-fishing gear and try your luck in the Redbank Creek, or simply take a walk along its banks. Play target golf, horseshoes, or take advantage of the 30-foot–by-60-foot athletic court to practice your jump shot or volleyball serve.

The 8,500-acre Cook Park National Forest is nearby. The area is famous for its old growth forest, once referred to as the "Black Forest." Cook Park's "Forest Cathedral" of magnificent lofty hemlocks and white pines is a National Natural Landmark. Along the eastern border of the park, canoeing and rafting on the Clarion River is a favorite pastime.

INNKEEPERS:	Pam and David Henderson
ADDRESS:	518 Bauer Road
	Summerville, Pennsylvania 15864
TELEPHONE:	(814) 856-3480; (800) 905-6647
E-MAIL:	info@thehouseattheendoftheroad.com
WEBSITE:	www.houseattheendoftheroad.com
ROOMS:	2 Suites; Private baths
CHILDREN:	Unable to accommodate
PETS:	Not allowed

Miniature Lemon Cheesecake Tarts

Makes 4 to 6 Servings

12	whole graham crackers, crushed
7	tablespoons unsalted butter, melted
1	(8-ounce) package cream cheese
$\frac{1}{3}$	cup sugar
1	egg
2	tablespoons sour cream
2	teaspoons lemon juice
$\frac{1}{2}$	teaspoon vanilla

Preheat oven to 375°F. Combine graham cracker crumbs and melted butter. Firmly press mixture into bottom and sides of cups in a mini tart/muffin pan.

Stir cream cheese and sugar until smooth. Beat in egg, sour cream, lemon juice, and vanilla. Fill each graham cracker lined muffin cup about ¾ full. Bake for 10 minutes until filling puffs slightly. Cool.

Pennsylvania

Classics

Amish Friendship Bread

The idea is very simple. A friend gives you a cup of yeast culture (also known as "starter"), and a copy of instructions. Following the instructions carefully for 10 days will result in 4 new cups of starter. Always use glass or plastic bowls and wooden or plastic spoons for this recipe.

You use one cup to make bread, one cup to start a new cycle and give a cup, with instructions, to two of your friends.

Starter (Do not refrigerate):

3	cups milk
3	cups sugar
3	cups flour

Day 1 – Mix 1 cup milk, 1 cup sugar, and 1 cup flour
Days 2-4 – Stir each day
Day 5 – Add 1 cup milk, 1 cup sugar, and 1 cup flour
Days 6-9 – Stir each day
Day 10 – Add 1 cup milk, 1 cup sugar, and 1 cup flour

Put 1 cup of mixture into three separate containers. Give to two friends and keep one for yourself as a starter. With remaining 1 cup of starter, make your Amish Friendship Bread.

Bread:

⅔	cup oil
2	cups flour
1	cup sugar
3	eggs
1½	teaspoons baking soda
1½	teaspoons cinnamon
1½	teaspoons salt
1½	teaspoons baking powder
1	cup starter

Mix all ingredients and add to starter. Combine well. Pour mixture into 2 loaf pans or 1 bundt cake pan that has been greased and floured. Bake at 350 for 45 to 50 minutes. You can also add raisins, blueberries, nuts, apples, bananas, etc. if you desire. Yield 2 loaves or 1 cake.

Shoofly Pie

When a shoofly pie is removed from the oven to cool, the sticky, sugary molasses that rises to the surface is a magnet for flies that must be constantly shooed away. This may be why this Pennsylvania Dutch specialty is called shoofly pie. In the late winter and early spring, the Pennsylvania Dutch colonists were left with a meager supply of ingredients with which to bake. Oftentimes, flour, molasses, and lard were all they had. Shoofly pie may have been created with these few reserves and a bit of resourcefulness. Today, shoofly pie has evolved to include a few more ingredients but is basically the same people-pleasing sweet treat Pennsylvanians have enjoyed for years.

Crumb mixture:
$1\frac{1}{2}$ cups flour
1   teaspoon baking powder
$\frac{1}{2}$ cup sugar
$\frac{1}{8}$ cup shortening

Liquid mixture:
$\frac{1}{2}$ cup hot water
$\frac{3}{4}$ teaspoon soda
$\frac{1}{2}$ cup corn syrup molasses

1   8- or 9-inch unbaked pie shell

Preheat oven to 350°F. Combine the four ingredients of the crumb mixture, using hands to work into crumbs. Set aside 2-3 tablespoons of the crumb mixture.

Combine the three ingredients of the liquid mixture, and fold the crumb mixture into the liquid.

Pour mixture into the pie shell and sprinkle with the remaining crumb mixture. Bake for 40 minutes.

Geographical Index of Bed & Breakfasts

Recipe Index

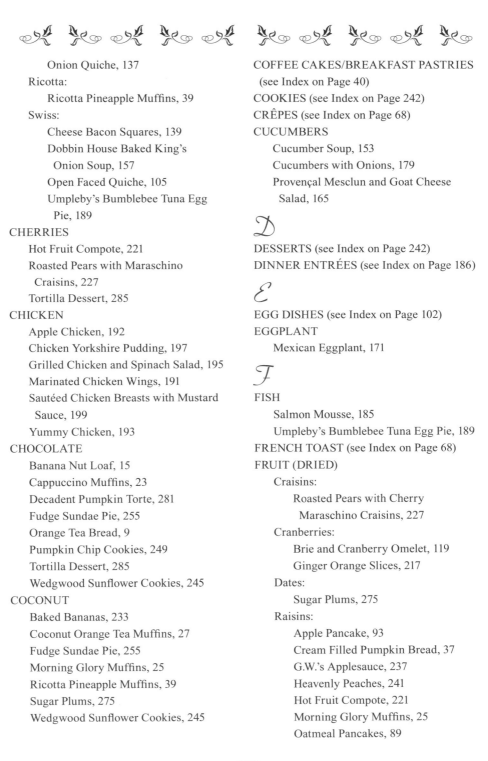

The Bed & Breakfast Cookbook Series

Collect all of the books from the Award-Winning B&B Cookbook Series.

Entertain with ease and flair!
Bed &Breakfasts from across the nation share their best and most requested recipes.

California Bed and Breakfast Cookbook
Book #5 in the series / 127 California B&B's and Country Inns
$19.95 / 328 pages / ISBN 1-889593-11-7

Colorado Bed & Breakfast Cookbook
Book #1 in the series / 88 Colorado B&B's and Country Inns
$19.95 / 320 pages / ISBN 0-9653751-0-2

New England Bed & Breakfast Cookbook
(CT, MA, ME, NH, RI, & VT)
Book #6 in the series / 107 New England B&B's and Country Inns
$19.95 / 320 pages / ISBN 1-889593-12-5

North Carolina Bed & Breakfast Cookbook
Book #7 in the series / 70 North Carolina B&B's and Country Inns
$19.95 / 320 pages / ISBN 1-889593-08-7

Pennsylvania Bed & Breakfast Cookbook
Book #8 in the series / 69 Pennsylvania B&B's and Country Inns
$19.95 / 304 pages / ISBN 978-1889593-18-0

Texas Bed & Breakfast Cookbook
Book #3 in the series / 70 Texas B&B's and Country Inns
$19.95 / 320 pages / ISBN 1-889593-07-9

Virginia Bed & Breakfast Cookbook
Book #4 in the series / 94 Virginia B&B's and Country Inns
$19.95 / 320 pages / ISBN 1-889593-04-1

Washington State Bed & Breakfast Cookbook
Book #2 in the series / 72 Washington B&B's and Country Inns
$19.95 / 320 pages / ISBN 1-889593-05- 2

Coming Soon: *Georgia Bed & Breakfast Cookbook* **(Fall, 2007)**

The Bed & Breakfast Cookbook Series Order Form

3005 Center Green Drive, Suite 220, Boulder CO 80301
800-258-5830 or www.bigearthpublishing.com

PLEASE SEND ME:	PRICE	QUANTITY
CALIFORNIA BED & BREAKFAST COOKBOOK	$19.95	_____
COLORADO BED & BREAKFAST COOKBOOK	$19.95	_____
NEW ENGLAND BED & BREAKFAST COOKBOOK	$19.95	_____
NORTH CAROLINA BED & BREAKFAST COOKBOOK	$19.95	_____
PENNSYLVANIA BED & BREAKFAST COOKBOOK	$19.95	_____
TEXAS BED & BREAKFAST COOKBOOK	$19.95	_____
VIRGINIA BED & BREAKFAST COOKBOOK	$19.95	_____
WASHINGTON STATE BED & BREAKFAST COOKBOOK	$19.95	_____

SUBTOTAL: $ _____

Add $5.00 for shipping for 1st book, add $1 for each additional book $ _____

TOTAL ENCLOSED: $ _____

SEND TO:

Name_____

Address_____

City_____State_____Zip_____

Phone_____A gift from:_____

We accept checks and money orders. Please make checks payable to Big Earth Publishing.

Please charge my ☐ VISA ☐ MASTERCARD ☐ AMEX ☐ DISCOVER

Card Number_____Expiration Date_____